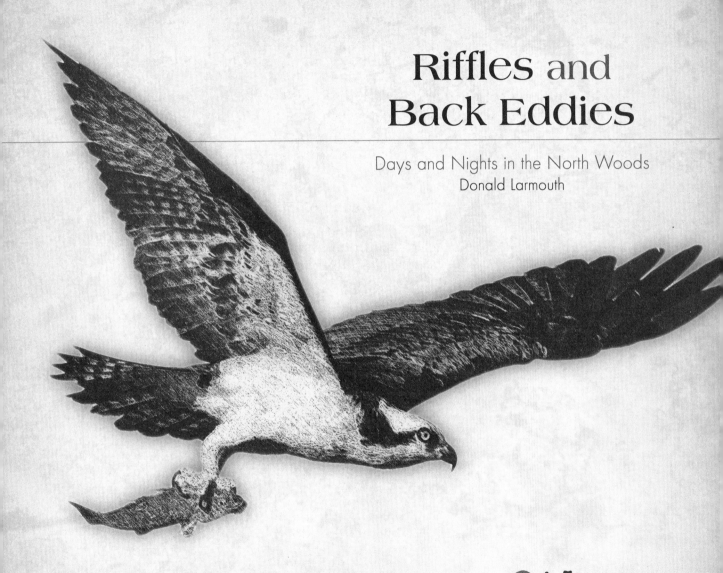

Riffles and Back Eddies

Days and Nights in the North Woods
Donald Larmouth

9th
street
publishing

154 N. Broadway
Green Bay, WI 54303

Riffles and Back Eddies

Days and Nights in the North Woods

For more information and copies of
this book, please contact:
www.9thstreetpublishing.com

Copyright ©2013 by Donald Larmouth

Published by:
9th Street Publishing
154 N. Broadway, Green Bay, WI 54303

Cover Design and Layout by: Prophit Marketing

www.prophitmarketing.com

Manufactured in the United States of America

Portions of this book were originally printed in:

Atlantic Salmon Journal

Fly Fisher

Fly Fishing and Tying Journal

Lake Superior Steellhead Association Annual

Salmon Trout Steelheader

Wisconsin Great Outdoors

I would like to thank the following: Dean Bortz, of Wisconsin's Great Outdoors, who gave me the opportunity to practice and develop a more open narrative style; Tim Landwehr and Charlie Piette of Tight Lines Fly Shop, who reviewed the manuscript; Rob Fordyce and Flip Pallot for introducing me to Salt Water fishing; Jim Wiersma who is the epitome of a good fishing buddy; and most of all to my wife, Judy, whose insistence, patience and hard work encouraged me to write this book; and those others without whose support it would have remained only a dream.

Don Larmouth
November 2012

Thanks to Robert and Kelly Walters,
Rachel Mittelstaedt and Joe Kiedinger
for their contributions to the
production of this book.

Table of Contents

Riffles
and
Back Eddies

Days and Nights in
the North Woods

Foreword

i

This collection of stories began with an invitation from Dean Bortz, a former student of mine at the University of Wisconsin-Green Bay, to write a fishing column for *Wisconsin's Great Outdoors*, a weekly outdoors newspaper that he began with high hopes but ultimately did not survive the forces of the market. Dean telephoned me in the midst of the usual piles of academic work and asked me if I would consider writing a biweekly column. At first I was not inclined to do it, assuming that he wanted a series of "how to/ where to" articles.

Responding to his assurances that he wanted outdoor narratives and recollections in the old style, "like the ones you told after class," I submitted a few possibilities and was pleasantly surprised that they were accepted. Even more gratifying were the many kind letters and telephone calls I received from readers of the column, which was called "Riffles and Back Eddies."

I chose this title to suggest that the content would be low-key and unimportant in the grander scheme of things—a collection of small stories about small events and (mostly) small fish.

I

Encounters

Boiling Up

It was one of those brutal early April mornings in northern Wisconsin when you wonder why on earth you decided to go steelhead fishing. Snow was still hip deep in the woods and more was falling in hard, wind-driven pellets. My rod guides were icing up and so were my fingerless wool gloves. The river itself seemed to be congealing between the snow banks as if it meant to thicken into ice, while its gray-green water pressed like an insistent hand against my waders. As the snow rattled against my parka hood, I had barely enough feeling left in my fingers to strip in the line and make yet another cast, shooting the bright orange and white fly up and across, then high-sticking the line and feeling for the occasional tick-tick of the split shot as it washed downstream among the boulders and gravel of the stream bed.

Finally I just had to get out and warm up. I reeled in and waded to the bank, tripping and stumbling several times, clumsy with the cold. Once out of the water, I looked around to see if there was enough dead wood close by for a fire. After scraping away the snow to make a fireplace, I opened my Duluth pack and found matches, a package of fire-starter tablets, a metal cup, and a tea pail. Inside the pail I had a dozen tea bags, a spoon, and sugar.

Shuffling through the snow, I made my way to a spruce tree and pulled off a few handfuls of dry twigs, piled them around the fire-starter, then broke up some larger twigs and dead branches from a blowdown a few yards farther away. Several minutes later I had enough wood for a decent fire. I lit the fire-starter tablet and watched as the flames moved eagerly upward through the tinder, popping and snapping among the spruce twigs. Smoke began to rise, only to be swept by another gust of wind. The little fire held its own, and soon the larger sticks were aflame as well.

I dipped out some water, propped up a dingle stick, and hung the tea pail just above the fire. As I waited for it to boil, I rubbed my weather-beaten hands together in the welcome heat, taking care not to get too close and singe my waders.

As if signaled by the smoke, several other anglers waded out of the river. Without a word they began to gather around the fire. Then, one by one, they propped up their rods against a bare moose maple and shuffled away to find more firewood. I could hear dry branches cracking as they were kicked and broken up. As if in a long-practiced ritual, each man brought back an offering of wood. Gradually the fire grew larger and more friendly. The tea pail began to steam, while other pairs of red and shivering hands stretched out toward the flames.

Huddled in a half circle, we were all silent at first; then someone ventured, "Pretty cold." There was a growl of agreement.

Someone else asked. "Anybody do any good?"

A man I recognized as an old hand on the river said he had taken one earlier, and we could see a broad tail sticking out from the large back pocket of his vest.

"Nice one," someone said, his voice muffled by a heavy scarf.

Another man said he caught two the day before, but was skunked today.

The water in the blackened pail finally came to a boil, and I tossed in a couple of tea bags. By now there were six of us standing around the fire.

I said, "I only have one cup, but there's lots of tea. Anybody else got a cup or something?"

Others reached into their parkas or vests, and the inventory of cups grew to four.

I filled each cup with tea, put out the sugar and a spoon, and soon pairs of reddened hands were clasped around the steaming cups. Someone passed around some sticks of jerky. As I poured refills the cups moved from hand to hand, and the tea pail was soon empty. I stepped away from the fire to fill it again.

As we began to thaw out, the grunts and nods of Ice Age men gave way to more lively conversation. One man began to tell how he lost a good fish up near the head of the run, deep down in the slab rocks, and another said you had to get moving downstream if you hooked a fish in there. A man with a large red beard told of following a steelhead across the river, only to break off in a sweeper. All of us had similar experiences—funny how we talked more about fish lost than fish landed.

The conversation then turned to yarn, Corkies, spawn bags, single eggs and other baits and lures. Soon plastic boxes were dug out and opened to show different colors, shapes and sizes. One man said he had good luck with bright green yarn, and soon we each had a few pieces to go with our other colors.

Then, as if green were a kind of signal, the group began to break up. We retrieved our rods and moved back toward the river. I kicked some snow into the fire, which was pretty well burned out anyway—hurrying a little, the way I always do when other fishermen are about and doing.

I waded back to my position in the run, unhooked the yarn fly where it had frozen to the rod, and began to cast. Upstream another angler hooked up, and I could see his long rod bending to powerful surges.

A few minutes later there was another hookup across the river, and the red-bearded angler splashed downstream, trying to hold the fish away from the sweeper.

I cast my fly up and across as I had done hundreds of times before, lifting the rod to feel for the familiar tick-tick of the split shot over the boulders, down deep where it had to be. It was hard to concentrate with action going on around me. Upstream a fresh-run steelhead had been lifted shining and thrashing in a net. Wading in waist deep, the red-bearded angler made it around the sweeper's dead limbs and struggled to beach his fish on a gravel bar.

Once again the snow pelted my parka hood as I settled into my familiar cast and drift routine. Then my rod lifted automatically to a sudden pull. I too had a fish on, a dim flash of silver in the swirling current. Turning to follow its run downstream, I glanced back at the smoking embers of our fire.

Why do we go steelhead fishing in April? Was it the silver sides and gun-metal blue back of the fish I brought to hand on the icy gravel? No fish is more beautiful than a fresh-run steelhead born wild and grown to perfect maturity untouched by human hands until our brief encounter. But it wouldn't be the same without the smoke from the warmup fire, the stark black tracery of bare alder limbs over white snowbanks, or my now wordless companions, faces hidden by their parkas, their shoulders hunched against the wind, legs braced against the gray-green flow of the river.

Crouching over my fish as she lay on the gravel, I looked upstream again. The red-bearded angler caught my glance and lifted his rod skyward in salute. I returned the gesture, following the unwritten rules of an invisible code. Then I lifted the steelhead a few inches off the gravel, looking at her a moment longer. She was a wild fish, no marks, her maturing roe still tight. There was no question of what to do next. I held her in the current until she kicked away and disappeared.

The Fly-Tier

The afternoon was overcast, with light winds and a hint of humidity—ideal conditions for a mayfly hatch. I suppose every fly fisherman lives for those golden interludes when mayflies emerge, the swallows and flycatchers dip and dart, and the river is pockmarked with eager rises. After a cold spring, the hatches were not spread out as usual. They were late and bunched together. As I began to set up my tackle, I knew it might be hard to figure out what fly to use.

As I worked upstream, a few pale grayish tan mayflies began to show, so I tied on a Gray Fox dry fly and covered the first good rise I saw. Emerging nymphs were struggling to break the surface film, and as the fly floated down untouched, I had already changed my mind about my choice, stripped it in, and tied on a no-hackle fly instead, something that would float awash and might look more like the emergers.

The next cast proved this was a good guess, and I tightened to a 12 –inch brown trout, fat from heavy feeding. I moved further upstream with greater confidence, covered another rise, and soon released another trout about the same size—good ones for this stretch.

As I waded through the shallow riffle to the next pool, I saw another angler sitting on the bank, hunched over with his back toward me. Before him, in the flat water above the tailout, emergent mayflies floated down, their upright wings tipping from side to side as light puffs of wind swept over them. Among them several trout were rising steadily, almost at the angler's feet.

Since he was already working the pool, I would have to go around him, but I decided to watch for a while. It was so perfect—a smooth current ideal for a drag-free drift, a good hatch, and several rising fish. He glanced up quickly; then turned back to whatever he was doing. At first I assumed he was selecting a fly, but as the minutes ticked by, he made no move to the water.

My own approach would have had me flailing in all directions, trying to cover every rising fish, so I couldn't imagine what had so absorbed his attention. Finally I waded to the bank and pushed through the undergrowth, staying well away from the pool.

"Looks like a nice hatch," I said. "Do any good so far?"

The angler turned, peering suspiciously over his half-frame glasses, and I spoke quickly to reassure him. "I'm going on upstream. There's another good pool around the corner."

He looked up again, more friendly this time. "I'm just about ready. It's a *Stenonema fascum* hatch, size #14, but there are some *subvaria* duns out there too." He nodded toward a piece of insect netting stretched over his landing net, which lay beside him. "I collected a few."

Moving a bit closer, I realized he was not putting on a fly or a new leader—he was tying a fly. He had a neat little hand-held vise, and spread all around him in the matted grass lay several plastic envelopes of dubbing, hackles, feathers, and hooks. I could see he was in the process of winding a hackle.

"Oh, damn!" he said, as the hackle broke off and unwound in a loose spiral. He reattached his hackle pliers and tried to wind on the hackle again. Apparently he didn't get a very good grip, because the hackle stem broke off again. Smiling grimly, he unwound the tying thread a few turns, let the bobbin dangle, and reached for a packet of hackles. He selected a new one, held it up to the light, and deftly tied it in place.

All this while, several handsome trout continued to rise to the mayflies drifting down the current. The angler knew this as well as I, and I dared not interrupt his concentration as he wound the hackle and whip-finished the fly.

"There!" he said, holding up his creation. Then he rolled to his feet and reached for the fly rod propped against a blowdown behind him. As he stood up, I saw he was wearing a large vest stuffed with fly boxes, but apparently nothing they contained was suitable for this occasion. Flipping down a magnifier clipped to his hat, he tied on the new fly and spritzed it with the floatant. Then he carefully placed his vise and all his materials in a canvas pouch and slid it into the back of his vest.

He seemed to have forgotten I was there, and I said nothing as he moved the water's edge, stripped line off his reel, stepped quietly into the shallows, and began to false-cast. I decided it was time to move on, not wishing to distract him at this critical moment. I watched as he worked his way out into the pool, still false-casting.

"Very impressive," I thought. "The guy comes to the river, sees what is going on, and whips up a fly on the spot. Now he should really nail 'em." I was admiring and envious of such expertise. It made my own fishing seem clumsy and haphazard. I started upstream to the next pool, then looked back one last time.

The fly-tying angler was no longer false-casting. Instead, he was staring upward. His backcast was hung up in a leaning spruce tree, well above the water and far out of reach. He tugged on the line and shook the rod for several minutes, which brought down a sprinkling of twigs and needles, but not the fly. Meanwhile, several good trout continued to rise all around him, ignoring his predicament.

Finally he broke off, and with the heavenward look of a martyred saint, he waded ashore and leaned his now flyless rod against the blowdown. Then he spread out his fly-tying kit, sat down among his envelopes of materials, and picked up his vise once again.

It must take real commitment to be an expert.

Class Reunion

The river was running high, and as I waded up the first riffle, I realized the relentless push of the heavy current would wear me out long before the evening rise. Spey-casting two wet flies downstream would be easier and still effective. With no hatch in sight, the trout would be feeding opportunistically—prime targets for a well-placed wet fly.

Giving in to the march of time and the laws of physics, I re-rigged with two wet flies and began to work downstream instead. But there was a nagging little voice inside, reminding me that in my youth I would have ploughed upstream regardless, making it a test of strength and skill, like shooting a rapids instead of portaging.

Then a good trout grabbed the Coachman dropper on the second drift, and I forgot my unsteady legs and other infirmities in the excitement of bringing it to net—a well-marked brown trout, nearly 14 inches. I waded into the slack water to release it and had the satisfaction of feeling it push out of my hand after a few moments' rest.

Moving down the foam-speckled run, I soon had another hit but missed the fish. I tried several more drifts but it wouldn't come again, so I moved along toward the tailout. As the current quickened, I lifted the long rod to skitter the dropper in the surface film, drawing it upstream and letting it drop back in front of a big boulder, where the water pushed its way upstream and formed a cushion –a good spot for a fish to rest and watch for food.

Another trout took the tail fly, a Dark Cahill, as it swung past the cushion. I pulled him out of the main current before he could get organized, got him coming, and quickly had him in the net—another good one, not so big as the first, but a chunky 12 inches.

No hits through the fast water, but at the head of the next run I released two small trout and then a ten-inch brookie—just a remnant of what had once been a strong brook trout population. With deeper water ahead, I cut off the Dark Cahill and put on a weighted caddis pupa. The rise and swing of a wet fly can suggest the movement of an emerging caddis, and I thought the extra weight would get the flies down. Peering over my glasses, I was again reminded of my advancing years as I squinted to poke the tippet though the hook eye, but I also had the confidence brought on by a busy hour and a few good fish.

As I turned to cast again, I saw another angler working upstream toward me, pushing hard against the heavy current, his fly line darting out and back like a striking snake. He was a big guy, and his rod looked like a willow switch in his large, strong hand. He moved steadily upstream, casting efficiently with no wasted motion, his casts curling out, the rod tip following the downstream drift, then a roll to lift the fly, flick-flick, and another cast was on its way. Just the way it should be done, I thought.

I hesitated, then decided to roll out a short cast before backing out of the water to let him through. I swung the rod in a small arc, laid the line across and downstream, then mended the slack to sink the flies deep. I could just make out the Coachman's white wing as the flies settled, then it suddenly disappeared.

I set the hook and had another good one throbbing against the long rod. The reel stuttered briefly in protest, but then the fish turned out of the main current. A few minutes later he was in the net—another bronze-colored brown trout, the caddis pupa stuck firmly in the hinge of his jaw.

"I see you haven't lost your touch, Professor!" boomed a voice.

Bending over the landing net, I looked up momentarily, then turned again to unhook the trout. After slipping the fish back, I straightened, looking more intently at the bulky shape silhouetted against the sun. The shape was familiar, the voice even more so, but I couldn't put a name to the broad face behind the sunglasses.

"You taught me to cast, out at the university," he said, and then I remembered him. At that time he had one of those multi-piece pack rods, the kind that seem to have a metal ferrule every eight inches.

I brought along a 9-foot graphite fly rod, and after I showed him the basic casting stroke, I handed it over. Two "casts" and I leaped in to rescue my precious rod from certain destruction. Like many beginners, he thought he could get the line out with sheer strength. When it didn't happen, he cast all the harder—and with him, that meant really hard. The line whistled back and forth and snapped menacingly, and the practice fly disappeared from the leader.

We gradually worked through the basics of the cast, and as he began to get the idea, he became convinced there was some magic in my outfit that was absent from his own. This required diplomacy. There was a lot wrong with his rod, but I knew many would-be anglers who spent hundreds of dollars on rods and tackle and still couldn't cast. To spare him this frustration, I picked up his pack rod and began to work out line. It had a soft, wobbly action, but I soon found a rhythm and laid out a few short casts—enough to show him it was the technique more than the equipment.

Now, many years later, here he was again, his casting far advanced from that first lesson on the university lawn. He had become a skilled fly fisherman, and he extended his hand as he waded across through the heavy current. "I guess this is a class reunion," he said, with a bone-crunching handshake. "More like the final exam," I replied, "and it looks like you'll pass."

The Loon and the Eagle

It was one of those bright, hot early summer days that had me wishing I had decided to fish a shaded stream instead of standing in my little johnboat fishing a clear trout pond. The surface was flat, the air was still and everything else was dead quiet. Even the birds had taken time out.

The morning's fishing had been good over the shoals, which showed up bright green and amber in the sunlight. While I normally cast blind for trout in lakes, this time I could see good fish cruising, turning now and then to grab something invisible to me. There wasn't anything hatching that I could see, but I had persuaded a couple of good rainbows and a brook trout to take my olive chironomid, sunk just under the surface on a long, fine tippet. (Truth to tell, I had also broken one off on the take – a "zing-snap!" for which rainbows in particular are noted.)

For a while, the trout had been cruising nearer the surface, like the "gulpers" in Hebgen Lake out in Montana, and it was possible to spot a fish, make a cast ahead, and get a good pull if everything went right. That's why I was still standing in my johnboat instead of sitting like a sensible person, even though the trout were now a lot deeper.

I had almost made up my mind to fold it up and wait until evening when I saw a loon pop up across the little bay. There were quite a few loons in the neighborhood, and they seemed to prefer the trout lakes. Maybe the hunting was better for them in the clean water, or maybe they just like trout better than other fish. (I can understand that.) I've noticed that ospreys like the clear lakes too, but then, good visibility is critical for their success.

I looked away from the loon, retrieved my little chironomid, and made another cast, letting the fly sink deeper on the long 5X tippet, then creeping it up very slowly, almost vertically, hoping that one of the cruising fish would notice its tiny movements and take it.

I should have been concentrating on the floating part of the leader, but I glanced down, alongside the boat, which was anchored at both ends so it wouldn't swing. The white anchor lines showed up plainly, and I could see the bow anchor sitting half buried in the bottom muck, ten feet down.

Then I saw the loon, swimming strongly about four feet down. It passed right under the boat, then turned hard right, graceful and swift like a seal. I had never seen an adult loon swimming underwater before, its huge gray feet churning, its wings pressed tight to its body. It was so close I could see the necklace of white spots around its neck, which was thrust straight out. The loon turned hard left, and there was a flurry of movement I couldn't follow, but I saw a silver flash in the water and realized the loon had struck a trout. Then it disappeared into the deeper water.

I don't know why the loon turned away, but I could see the trout plainly, its white belly and silver sides bright against the green of the bottom, and it began to rise slowly to the surface, probably 20 feet from the boat.

Then I heard a raspy whistle, looked up, and saw an eagle gliding just over the treetops, the sun bright on its white head and tail. It whistled again— one of the most stirring sounds of the North – and lighted in an old jackpine across the bay.

The eagle's yellow beak was pointed directly at the stricken trout, which was now just below the surface. Its bright, baleful eye was fixed on the feebly moving fish, and I realized the eagle wanted to pick it off. I watched and watched, motionless in the johnboat. I was close—perhaps too close for the eagle to come. I tried not to look directly at the trout. It was a good one, maybe 16 inches.

We were all a frozen tableau – the trout, the eagle and myself, against the flat calm of the pond. Then the eagle swept down from its perch, and I thought for sure it was going to snatch the trout. But it flew over several feet above my head and landed again in a bush behind me. Perhaps it was afraid. After all, it wasn't that long ago that people shot at hawks and eagles—and some still do.

I didn't dare turn around, but after several more minutes of waiting I was growing unsteady, so I sat down very slowly. I was afraid I might tip the little boat. Then I heard the rush of wings sudden and close and felt the hair rise on the back of my neck.

The eagle swept past me at eye level, plucked the trout from the surface with one talon, like a dowager taking a sugar cube at high tea, and was gone over the tree line.

Some minutes later, rowing in, I remembered I had brought my camera.

Chironomids

The pond was flat calm in the summer heat, perfectly mirroring the treeline—no swirls, no rises, nothing but the spiraling of whirligig beetles and the footprints of water striders in the quiet shallows. This unrevealing surface concealed an abiding mystery: what were the trout feeding on? Or were they feeding at all? Were there any good ones left after the early season assault on the spring ponds?

A discouraged angler rowed in as I rigged up, momentarily distorting the perfect mirror of the pond. To my unspoken question he replied, "Not a hit since early morning. They just aren't biting today."

I murmured sympathetically, secretly glad to have the pond to myself. Then I stepped into my float tube and finned my way to a dropoff. I anchored just off a weedy shoal and straightened an extra-long fine leader. I could see several fresh pupal shucks on the surface—a good sign. Tying on a tiny olive chironomid pupa, I made a cast to the deep water waited as the fly and leader sank.

Some minutes later, in the middle of a slow retrieve, I saw the line move, tightened up, and a good trout burst through the calm surface like a rock hurled through a window. It was a thick, prime rainbow, nearly 17 inches and fat from heavy feeding, and it jumped twice more before coming to the net.

Like the man in the rowboat, I used to think trout had meal times, just like people. The pond was either pocked with rises from feeding fish or it was dead quiet. Now I know better. Although there are quiet times, except for extreme temperatures or the distractions of spawning, trout are usually feeding. It's how they make a living. At times, a certain type of food may attract their attention and ours—something visible like emerging mayflies, flying ants tumbling to the surface, the dance of egg-laying caddis—which prompts us to "match the hatch." The rest of the time, their feeding is invisible to us.

For a while I used a stomach pump to find out what the trout were eating. The most recently ingested food was obvious, sometimes still alive. But everything else was a hodgepodge of nymphs, snails, scuds, and chironomids, or midge pupae, the latter often looking like an olive-colored paste.

Reading more about lake ecology, I learned chironomids were often the most abundant and available food item, particularly the pupae, which rise vertically from the bottom sediments, often in deep water, to emerge as tiny two-winged flies similar to mosquitoes. This was interesting but no help until I fished several of British Columbia's Kamloops trout lakes. The first few days my usually reliable Muddler Minnows and Woolly Buggers failed miserably, while other anglers fishing from small prams caught big silver rainbows. All the while I saw nothing break the surface. Now and then one of them would stand up, false cast several times, lay out a cast, and sit down again. Using floating lines and long leaders, 16 feet or more, they cast their tiny chironomid imitations, waited several minutes as they sank deep, then s-l-o-w-l-y inched them toward the surface. When I finally got the idea, used the right fly, and followed their example, business was brisk.

It's hard to imagine large trout swimming through clouds of chironomids, inhaling dozens of pupae, but in many lakes this is exactly what they do, the only evidence the white-gilled shucks of the pupae that made it through the unseen carnage to the surface. Trout can grow very big on such tiny insects because they are so abundant and they don't have to spend much effort to catch them.

As I released the trout, I heard a commotion behind me. I turned in the float tube and saw two young fellows launching a johnboat, dragging the protesting metal hull over the rocks and dumping it in with a crash. After they loaded up the coolers, tackle boxes, rods, bobbers, and a radio, they cranked the motor and headed straight for me.

"Whatcha usin?" the guy running the motor shouted, shifting into neutral and tipping back the visor on his cap.

The other one was wearing cutoffs and a "Get Naked" T-shirt. He grinned and chimed in, "We seen ya get a nice one."

Bobbing up and down in their wash, I felt a little foolish looking up at them from my float tube as they drifted closer.

"A chironomid," I replied.

"Huh?"

I tried to explain. "Midges, little flies that come up from the bottom. They look like this." I held up the leader tippet, exhibiting the #14 fly, just a long, thin abdomen and a little clump of peacock herl and white ostrich herl at the head. It looked like an elongated comma.

"Shoot!" (or something like that) said the one running the motor. "I can't even see it." Then to his friend, "Let's go over by the point." He shifted the motor into reverse, and I bobbed in a blue cloud of exhaust fumes as they sputtered over to a marshy point about 30 yards away. A kingfisher rattled away from a dead snag as their anchor plunged overboard.

I watched them untangle their rods, bait up, and cast out their bobbers. I knew it was only a matter of time before the radio started blaring. As the lake settled into calm again, one of them caught a small trout, so they became more intent, and I made another hopeful cast.

As before, I let the chironomid pupa sink deep, then inched it upward in tiny hand-twist pulls, trying to ignore the other boat, hoping things below the surface would quiet down.

The attentiveness that follows a caught fish soon faded, and before long I heard a snap as a beer can was opened, soon followed by another. The radio started a few minutes later, wailing of honky-tonks and lost love, and two red-and-white bobbers lay immobile, embedded in the glassy surface.

Grimacing at the noise but not yet willing to leave, I made another cast to the deeper water, waited a few minutes for the fly to sink well down, and began a slow retrieve. It took a long time, but finally the leader butt twitched slightly, and I tightened to another good fish. Fly line leaped through the guides and the old Hardy reel began to screech.

"Fish on," I said—probably too triumphantly—trying not to look toward the anglers in the johnboat. Far out, another heavy rainbow boiled at the surface.

"Shoot!" said the one in the "Get Naked" T-shirt—or something like that.

II
Times

Ice-out

After a long week at the office, I was finally on my way north for Opening Day. It was already late afternoon by the time I had the canoe on the car, and it was a long drive to the landing—the "jumping-off place," as the old-timers of the canoe country call them.

The sun was down when I arrived, loaded the canoe, and set off. Normally I wouldn't paddle so far after dark, but the lake was long and narrow, the unbroken horizon of spruce trees outlining the shore. The night was calm, and I knew I could find the portage to the next lake, where I intended to camp and fish over the opening weekend. It had been a cold spring, and patches of snow still loomed white beneath the black and naked trees, showing up like tombstones in the dark. Momentarily distracted, I caught a crab with the paddle and splashed some water in my lap. The lake water was very cold, and I reminded myself that I would be in serious trouble if I got careless.

The afterglow in the west had disappeared before I was a third of the way down the lake. The surface was perfectly calm, eerily reflecting the glittering starlight. As I stopped to rest and let the canoe drift, the Northern Lights began to play—much more brightly than I would have expected in early May.

Soon the entire surface of the lake shimmered with the aurora. I couldn't separate the water from the sky, and when I began to paddle again, it seemed that I was paddling up among the stars themselves. Long ago Peter Pond, an early Canadian explorer, had written that on a cold night he could hear the Northern Lights fluttering like a flag in the wind. I heard nothing, but they certainly seemed close enough to hear. They swirled and danced, lifting and dropping like rose and green-tinted curtains in an open window.

As spectacular as it was, I was almost relieved when the aurora faded and a light breeze began to ripple the surface, sorting out the world once more into land, water, and air. I began to pull toward the narrow bay at the end of the lake. My eyes pried at the shoreline darkness, and finally I saw the logs of the landing ahead. The cold water lapped gently against them.

I realized it had dropped below freezing when I slipped on a thin skim of ice on the cross-log and almost fell headlong off the landing, but I managed to get the pack and canoe ashore without further mishap. I decided to carry my Duluth pack over the portage first, set up the tent at the campsite, then return for the canoe, confident no one else would be around this time of night.

The beam of my flashlight wove about the darkness, and last year's leaves, white with frost, crunched under my boots as I crossed the portage. Reaching the other end, I found the fire grate and dropped the pack. I retrieved the poles I had stacked at the campsite the year before, lashed them together in two V's, and put up the old poplin tent in a flat space between two jackpine trunks, as many had done before me.

As I snugged down the tent lines and fluffed up my sleeping bag, I noticed the unnatural quiet. The campsite was up the hill from a pebble beach, and with the soft westerly breeze, I should have heard the lapping of the lake water against the rocks. Reaching for the flashlight again, I walked down to the shore, shined the beam along the rocks, and discovered that the lake was completely iced in.

I decided then to leave the canoe at the other end of the portage until morning. If the lake stayed frozen, I would remain in camp and just carry my tackle to the opposite side of the portage and fish the other lake. With that out of the way, I slung the bear bag aloft between two trees, snuggled into my thick sleeping bag and fell asleep.

The next morning dawned cold and bright. My boots were stiff with cold, but after fumbling to pull them on and button up a wool cruiser jacket, I walked down to the lake. I saw that a sparkling blue lead had opened in the black ice, close to the rocky shore. The needle ice was tinkling like a wind chime as it crumbled in the water, and the lake began to boom and crack as the ice broke up. The tea in my thermos bottle was almost warm, so I drank a cup, ate a handful of raisins, and went back across the portage to pick up the canoe. I hurried along the frosty trail, because I had never seen the ice go out of a lake before. I also knew the lake trout might still be close to the reefs where they had spawned the previous fall.

When I returned, the lead had widened considerably, so I put the canoe in the water, paddled out to the edge of the ice floe, and rigged up a spinning rod with a sinker and an Al's Goldfish spoon. The light westerly breeze was just enough to allow me to drift slowly along the edge of the collapsing ice, working the spoon in lifts and drops. The six-pound test line enabled me to get down pretty well with a light sinker, and I soon hooked a small lake trout, which I released without removing it from the water.

All the while the lake boomed and groaned as the ice broke up. I thought it would be a slow process, but by noon more than half the lake had opened up, and the east shore was awash with the jingling needle ice. The wind continued light, and I worked the gold spoon up and down as I drifted into deeper water. But nothing took hold, and I finally paddled in for lunch.

Despite the bright sunlight it was still very cold, and I decided to build a midday fire to warm myself and boil up some fresh tea. Gathering the wood was enough work to get the blood moving again. I had spotted a dead pin cherry tree the year before, found it untouched, and decided I would have some high-class firewood—perfect for broiling coals, if I managed to catch a trout.

By early afternoon I had pretty well thawed out, so I put the canoe in the water again, paddled up against the wind a few hundred yards, and drifted back, working the spoon as before. Then I felt a strike, set the hook, and soon had a three-pound lake trout, a perfect size for the grate. The trout glistened on the cold bottom of the canoe, its gill covers slowly opening and closing, its orange fins bright against the aluminum.

I fished for another two hours, but the wind was cold off the lake, and though I was wearing almost every stitch of clothing I had, I finally had to give up and pull in. The trout was stiff and cold now, so were my fingers. I had to be very careful as I split the fish and sliced off a bright orange fillet.

The firewood from the dead pin cherry was everything I had hoped for, and I ate broiled lake trout and buttered rice and drank hot tea until I could hold no more. I hung the other half of the fish over a line stretched between two trees, confident that it would remain cold through the night.

Since there was still plenty of light, I slid the canoe back in the water. All the ice was gone except for the slush and needle ice which had piled up along the east shore. Had I arrived only a day later, I might never have imagined the noisy spectacle of ice-out. But the pressing business of the moment was fishing, so once again I began to drift, jigging the bright gold spoon and taking an occasional paddle stroke to move into new water.

It was almost sunset when I felt a bump as the spoon descended. I set hard and hooked up on a strong fish. The drag on the little spinning reel shrilled higher and higher as the trout plunged off of the reef into deep water. There was still a crisp breeze, and the canoe continued to drift eastward, away from the trout. But after several long minutes punctuated by more deep, head-shaking runs, I saw a stream of bubbles, and then the fish was at the surface. I lifted it aboard just as the canoe slid into the needle ice and heaving slush at the end of the bay. Had the fish made it to the ice, it might well have cut me off.

The lake trout wasn't all that big by North Country standards—about six pounds—but it was plenty of trouble on the light spinning outfit. Its mottled back and spotted sides faded gradually to a pale white belly, and its orange fins were edged with white, almost like a brook trout.

Suddenly cold and shivering from excitement, I paddled back to the campsite, cleaned the fish, and hung it up with the other one. Then I got the fire going again and warmed my hands in its glow. I had brought along a little celebratory flask of bourbon whiskey, so I toasted Opening Day, the lake, the trout, the Northern Lights, and drained it. I knew the liquor would actually make me colder, but it was a fine old bourbon, and it did feel very good going down.

The ensuing night was very cold. Once I got up and stepped outside the tent, hoping to see the aurora again, but I could see only a small slice of the sky through the trees. I walked down to the lakeshore and stood silent for a while, but there was nothing—no pink and green curtains, only the timeless wheeling of the stars. They were intensely bright and close, like they are in midwinter, and I could hear the remaining ice washing in and out against the rocks. It was too cold to watch for very long. Back in the tent, I hugged myself and shivered in my bag before dropping off to sleep.

The trout were frozen stiff when I checked them the next morning. The condensation from my breathing had gathered on the inside walls of the tent, so that it crunched and crackled when I took it down and folded it back into the packsack. I wrapped the trout in two plastic bags and laid them across the top of the folded tent, then buckled the pack flap down over them for the portage out.

I had planned to fish again in the morning, but the wind was rising from the north and low gray clouds scudded across the sky as I carried the canoe and pack across the portage. I knew it would be a cold, hard trip back down the lake to the jumping-off place. Overhead, a raven croaked unpleasantly, as if hoping that the wool-jacketed figure below him would suffer a deadly accident.

But you learn to be very careful when you travel alone in the canoe country, and though it was getting rough, I made it back down the lake to the take-out without incident, much to the raven's disappointment. As I lashed down the canoe for the long drive home, I noticed that the droplets of water had already frozen along the gunwales, and my fingers were stiff and sore from the paddle. I walked back to the gravel beach for a last look as snow began to fall from the low clouds, rattling against the hood of my anorak. The lake was now an unfriendly gray-green, and the rising wind drove flecks of foam from the top of the waves. Two more ravens flew overhead, sailing downwind, ever watchful.

"Here's to Opening Day," I said, squinting into the wind and gesturing an imaginary toast with an invisible flask.

Spring Football

For devoted Wisconsin Badger fans, "spring football" means the annual cycle of spring practices and scrimmages at Camp Randall Stadium, but to anglers it means a Lake Michigan brown trout—spotted silver and strong like an Atlantic salmon, but short and thick from heavy feeding on alewives and smelt.

When I bought my boat for inshore fishing, I rigged it with a mast and planer boards to spread the lines out, away from the wake, on the theory that the trout would spook from under the hull, swim out to the side, and see a lure as a snack en route. Fishing with long rods and light lines, we often saw a hooked fish leap far astern before the rod bent down in the rod-holder.

For a while it was exciting. The trout were handsomely marked and pulled like little bulls. I bought lures in many different sizes and colors, sharpened every hook, kept records of wind and weather, trolling speeds, depths— all the details. I enjoyed some success, but as time went on I also felt less and less like an angler. Rigging the lures, spreading the lines, watching the graph, the temperature gauge, the speed indicator, the planer boards—it was like setting an elaborate trap and waiting for some unlucky trout to spring it. With all the stuff between me and the lure, I didn't even get to feel the strike.

Finally I decided I had to re-engage myself in the fishing, a decision helped along by a heavy snowdrift in front of the garage. Chiseling through that frozen pile to get the boat out would be much harder work than tying a few flies, pumping up the float tube, and pulling on thick neoprene waders. With the unflagging optimism of the fly fisherman, I figured a streamer or a bucktail would be as effective as a Rapala. Besides, I had caught many trout from inland lakes on flies—what could be so different?

Thus I found myself standing on a snow-covered Lake Michigan beach in full regalia—float tube, fins, waders, PFD vest, fingerless gloves, and fly rod—a curiosity to trollers and hikers alike. The cold lake water moved uneasily, and so did I. The blue-green swells looked a lot bigger at eye level than they did from a trolling boat.

Even with thick fleece clothing under my waders, I could feel the penetrating chill of the 40-degree water, and as I sat down and kicked away from shore, the mild chop tossed annoying handfuls of icy water over the casting apron and up my sleeves. Once under way, I made a long cast with a slow-sinking line, stripped more line off the reel, and began to fin along, twitching the fly to give it more life. Fly fishermen don't troll, of course—they "mooch," which means the same thing but sounds more sophisticated, like "strike indicator" instead of "bobber." Whatever you call it, it's a good way to poke around and find the fish.

Nothing happened for a while, but the effort of kicking along helped me to stay warm—or so I told myself. But it was tiring, and finally I anchored along a deep shelf and began to cast. The water was clear, but I saw nothing—no smelt, no alewives, no trout, only the greenish-yellow of the limestone reef below.

The fly line was stiff from the cold and leaped up in wiry coils, when I cast, but eventually the old casting rhythm returned. All very well, but a half hour of casting brought no hits, so I pulled my anchor and began to mooch along again, trying different depths and retrieves. Then I changed to a spool with a faster-sinking line—no small feat with cold fingers. Across the bay, near the lighthouse, I could see a few trolling boats bristling with rods and trailing cobwebs of shiny monofilament and pairs of orange trolling boards.

I wasn't doing anything different—just the usual strip-strip-pause retrieve—when suddenly the fly line was yanked from my half-frozen fingers. The stiff coils sprang off the casting apron, and the mother of all knots gathered itself at the stripping guide. Luckily, nothing broke except the leader, and a football brown trout was now out there somewhere, wearing a new blue and white mustache.

The cold crept further into me as I untangled the line, furious at getting caught unawares. Alternately blowing on my fingers and cursing the snarl, I slowly got everything straightened out. It was another major project to tie on another tippet and a new bucktail, but I was finally ready for business again.

The wind had blown me inshore while I fumbled with my equipment, so I kicked my way out again, casting to the side, letting the fly swing and sink, retrieving it in short pulls as I finned backward into the wind. I was fired up now, but another frigid hour passed without a strike.

The new bucktail eventually became an object of suspicion, so I changed to a green and white feather streamer that might be more lively on the re-trieve. The feathers had an annoying habit of fouling under the hook bend, but the streamer looked good in the water, its painted eyes suggesting a frightened smelt or alewife. Hope springs eternal—especially when you've just tied on a new fly.

Drifting backward, I banged out another cast and let the fly drop and swing, the rod tip almost touching the water. I had just begun to retrieve when the fly line snapped tight. I didn't have to strike—the fish had set the hook and was yards away before I could react—but the rod was up, the line was clear, and backing screamed off the reel. Far away, a chunk of silver burst through the surface, and there weren't many turns left on the reel when it slowed. I like the sound my old Hardy reel makes when a fish runs, but this time I thought it would fly apart. Pumping and reeling, I gained almost all the backing before the next run, and then I knew I had the fish unless something went very wrong.

The trout didn't look all that big as it circled the float tube, but when I lifted it in the landing net, it was suddenly heavy like a piece of bright metal, about five pounds—just your average spring football.

How's that, sports fans?

Bass by Night

The Fourth of July is perhaps less a patriotic celebration than an excuse to head north to the lake and join thousands of others with the same idea: bring all the family, grandma, and the neighbor kids, swarm any available beach, go swimming, jet-skiing, or water-skiing, fire up the grill, and make as much noise as possible.

It wasn't exactly the Fourth of July, but everything else was the same when I arrived at the landing. Wet heads bobbed everywhere. There was a steady roar of motors, sailboards of many colors skimmed across the surface, and music poured from the juke box at the resort.

I parked the car, opened up my binoculars, and began to scan the shoreline. Some probably thought I was ogling the girls in bikinis, but I had a contour map of the lake, and I was laying out a plan. After locating a point with a brushy shoreline and a shallow weedbed in the crook of its arm, I launched the canoe and began to paddle, picking my way through the boats and sunburned bodies.

Moving slowly along, I tried to match the boat docks, stumps, logs, brushpiles, and other cover with the treeline so I could find them again after dark. The lake had a reputation for big bass, and this was going to be a night assault.

As the sun dropped to the horizon, campfires and bug-zapper lights winked on. Smoke and laughter rose from the grills, and almost every group had a radio going full blast. Several sunburned teenagers had erected a volleyball net, and every score was announced by shouts of triumph and shrieks of delight. A few stopped for a moment to shade their eyes and peer at the white-haired figure sitting alone in his canoe.

Anchoring near the end of the point, I rigged up my plug-casting outfit. The reel with its black braided line was old-fashioned, but it was harder to pick backlashes out of monofilament by feel. It may have been nostalgia, too, for this was the way my father and I fished for bass many years ago. In those days we tied the braided line directly to a snap-swivel, but as a concession to modern times, I added a 20-pound monofilament leader.

As in those long-ago years, I tied on a Jitterbug, although I could have started with a red-headed River Runt or a Johnson Silver Minnow with a pork frog. Those were our three basic choices then, and despite a dizzying multiplication of bass lures in the tackle shops and catalogues, I had found no reason to change since.

Near midnight the campfires and the cabin lights began to go out, but the beer sign at the resort was still on, and the juke box was still booming. That was bad. I needed silence as well as darkness to do business. I made a few casts to get used to the outfit again and brought the Jitterbug back with a series of wobbles and stops, trying to make it sound like something in trouble. I heard a thin smack, set the hook, and brought in a crappie. It was still too early for serious work.

Finally the beer sign went out, and except for the frogs the lake was quiet. The night life—the real night life—began to stir. A barred owl hooted back in the trees, and another owl (or maybe the same one) flew silently overhead. With a smile I remembered my father's Kentucky translation, "Ah cooks for mahself—who cooks fer you-all?" Far back in the darkness, near a cluster of flooded brush, I heard the crash of a good bass as it lunged after unseen prey—a frog, maybe, or a fat chub or sunfish.

I lifted the anchor and began to work down the shoreline. It was important to hear the plug land in the water and how it sounded on the retrieve, to tell if it had picked up weeds on the way back. My eyes pried at the dark, and I listened to the plug swimming across the surface.

The first strike came suddenly (at night they all do.) I jammed the rod into the water to keep the fish from jumping and reeled hard to get it clear of the weeds. It was a good one, and twice the old ivory reel handles rapped my knuckles. The bass surged back and forth along the gunwale, then a quick lift and it was in the canoe—a two-pounder, fat from heavy feeding.

I resisted the temptation to snap on the flashlight, which would have blinded me for several minutes. I got hold of the bass's lower jaw, felt around, and removed the hooks. Then I held it up, silhouetted against the stars, and put it back.

Easing down the shoreline again, I cast and backlashed. The plug crashed into the water a few yards from the canoe, and I began to pick at the tangle. It took a few minutes, but eventually I cleared it and reeled up. The next cast was better, landing just beyond a big stump—a denser blackness in the dark. "Bass, watch out!" I said half aloud, but there was no answering splash, and the Jitterbug gurgled its way back to the canoe unmolested.

The next cast rattled the plug among the bare and broken limbs of a half-submerged brushpile. I couldn't yank it free and had to paddle over to un-tangle it. A bass boiled out as the canoe scraped the branches, jumping several times as it churned through the shallows. They always sound really big when they do that—and some of them are.

A breeze came up as I approached a dock and an old white boathouse, so I silently lowered the anchor. Luckily, the owner had turned off the dock light. The whiteness of the boathouse door looked like a good target, but the first cast sailed too far and the Jitterbug bounced off into the water. That looked good, but the bounce had fouled the plug in the leader, so I reeled up and cast again.

This time the plug barely moved when a bass whopped it. Once again the rod was in the water and I was reeling hard to get the fish clear of the dock. This time I had an anchor rope to worry about, but after two slashing jumps the bass was in the canoe, thick-bodied and well over three pounds. Did the owner know such a fish lived under his dock?

This time I couldn't clear the hooks without a light, so I snapped on the flashlight, revealing the glowing eyes and pot belly of a good largemouth in prime condition, its tail almost completely healed from spawning. I had the light on only a few moments, but I had to wait several minutes before my night vision returned.

Working further along the shoreline, I picked up several more fish, and only two of them were less than a pound—good bass fishing anywhere. Finally I came around to the beach and the landing, now silent where hundreds of arms and legs had churned the water earlier, and made the first several "one last casts" near the dock.

The last bass to smash the Jitterbug wasn't any bigger than the others, but there was a special satisfaction in releasing it a few yards from the deserted boat ramp and a still smoldering grill.

They might have the day, I thought, but the bass and I, we own the night.

Time Machine

The portage trail rose steeply ahead of me, and I had to dig in my toes and tilt the canoe well back on my shoulders to get up the hill. Two paper birch trees grew close together a few yards beyond its crest, forming a convenient V, so I wedged the bow between them, slid out of my pack straps, and sat down for a breather. It had been cool out on the lake, but the air was hot and still in the woods.

I looked up at the thwarts to make sure that my rods were still firmly tied in, then sat down, dug my water bottle out of my packsack and took a long swig. A deerfly settled on my hand, undaunted by my bug dope, but I nailed it on the first swat, and no others discovered me.

As my ears stopped pounding and my breathing returned to normal, I pulled out my pocket notebook and scanned the previous day's pages. Four good smallmouth bass had come to a black Woolly Bugger and three more to a white hair bug during the day, and I had taken several more on my ol' reliable #11 Rapala just after dark. I had seen a mink, an otter, a pair of ospreys, an immature eagle, some hen mergansers and their half-grown ducklings, and several species of warblers and sparrows, most of which I couldn't identify from their late summer plumage.

I recalled one bass in particular. By some trick of light and shadow, I had seen him holding close under a fallen-in snag whose bare roots still gestured skyward from the steep bank. I could also see he was a very good one, well over three pounds. Anchoring the canoe, I picked up the fly rod and cast a deerhair bug close to the tree.

It was a lucky cast that turned the bug over well underneath, in the shadow of the trunk. The bass didn't move, and I let the bug sit there, floating awash and wiggling of its own accord. One little pop and the bass rocketed straight up through five feet of clear water, slammed the bug, and headed back down with all engines wide open.

It had been a touchy business to get him out from under the limbs of the snag, but I could see every move he made. When I released the fish a few minutes later, he went right back to the same spot, as if he were daring me to try that cast again. I could imagine his eyes glowing red in fury, as they had when I unhooked the bug and held him up in the sunlight to admire his bronze sides streaked with brown.

I could almost feel the bass in my hand again as I folded my notebook and leaned back against the birch trunk. The last couple of days had been very productive despite the warmth of late summer. I had seen some new country, had some time alone, and caught a fish I would remember for a long time.

Then, as the wind began to stir, I heard a car horn blow, long and insistently—no doubt some impatient family members honking to bring their hard-pressed dad back in from the lake. I could understand—it was a long way to the nearest drive-in.

The sound reminded me that I would only have to finish the carry and paddle another half mile to reach the take-out. The blatting of the horn was intrusive, and I was momentarily annoyed, but I realized that I could portage back down the hill and a few paddle strokes would put it out of my hearing—and a few more strokes would put it out of my mind.

I recalled another canoe excursion which began under a busy highway bridge a few blocks from my home. Paddling upstream, I passed suburban developments and farm country, and before long I was moving through quiet, heavily wooded bottom lands that probably hadn't changed in a generation, despite the hustle-bustle nearby. True, there wasn't any serious fishing to be had in that much abused river, but I was still drawn to the primordial even by watching a school of carp rolling and rooting in the shallows. I had seen a raccoon peering out at me from an overhead limb, just as his ancestors had probably peered at mine.

There were many other times when, simply by pushing the canoe through a narrows or making a short carry, I could reach water that was almost never fished, where the fishing was sometimes almost too easy to be interesting—even within a mile of heavily traveled, hard-fished lakes with a full complement of resorts, speedboats, and water-skiers.

Sitting there with my back against the birch, I remembered a film I saw called *Tarpon Country* in which the narrator described the modern outboard-driven skiff as a "time machine" that sped its anglers back into the Everglades wilderness and back in time, away from modern Miami skyscrapers, crowded beaches and bumper-to-bumper traffic to the primitive country of alligators, snail kites and tarpon.

Thanks to a guide who had grown up in south Florida, I had fished some of the same country by canoe, jumped several small tarpon and lost count of the snook we released. We had experienced the dark mangrove channels and backwaters as they must have been more than fifty years ago. Our only companion that day was a nine-foot alligator; the only sounds were the splashes of leaping mullet, the rifle-shot explosion of a snook crashing bait, the swish and crunch of the pushpole in the shallow water—and the constant menacing hum of millions of insect wings back among the leaves.

The car horn honked again from the parking lot, breaking once again into my afternoon reverie and prompting me to get up, put away my notebook, and shrug on my weatherbeaten packsack. As I lifted its bow from between the birches and settled the yoke on my shoulders, I realized that the canoe was my way of traveling back to the primitive—my time machine.

Night Sounds

It was yet another blue-sky day, hot and windy—unusual for early June in the north. After almost a month of dry weather there were fires in the north woods, with more yet to come. I had promised myself a walleyed pike or two before going home, but the prospects looked dim as I stood watching the whitecaps march down the channel.

I decided to come back at dark. It would be a long paddle on a moonless night, and rocks lurked just under the surface, but I knew a gravel shoal near a wooded island. In daylight it would be empty, but at night the walleyes might move out of the deeps to feed.

I returned with a hint of rosy afterglow in the west and launched the canoe. The hot wind had died away, and the swish and gurgle of each paddle stroke was amplified by the darkening shoreline. Bats fluttered soundlessly overhead, snapping at invisible insects.

Navigating by compass and the vague shapes of a familiar treeline, I finally saw the island, a denser blackness in the dark, like a ship at anchor. I let the canoe drift as I searched out the shoal and the weeds.

Feeling for bottom, I felt the anchor catch weeds, so I moved the canoe with a few quiet strokes, and this time found gravel and rubble. I let the canoe drift away from the anchor to give it purchase in the bottom, then drew it close again, tied off, and stowed the paddle. I rechecked my equipment— light spinning rod, six-pound test line, two feet of ten-pound test as a bite tippet, and a #11 Rapala. The plan was to fish the lure near the surface, nodding and twitching like an unlucky minnow.

As I placed my pliers and flashlight under my seat, the night sounds came closer. The canoe's approach had silenced the chorus of frogs in the woods, but now they croaked and chirped once more. An owl hooted a question in the gloom, and I heard something wading in the shallows. A faint whisper of wind began to stir, and I could hear the lapping of wavelets against the shoreline. Then the wind quieted again.

It was full dark when I made the first cast. Spinning tackle is risky at night, when unseen loops and spirals of line could tangle, so I felt the spool to make sure it was clear before each retrieve. I could hear the line whispering through the guides when I cast, but nothing bothered the plug on the first cast or the next five or six. So I reeled up and waited again. Pounding the water would be a mistake—if I dropped the plug right on a fish, everything would spook.

After ten minutes, I made several more casts, fanning them around, making sure to fish out each one. The bite tippet knot clicking through the guides told me to pick up and cast again. Occasionally I glimpsed the plug on the surface, but mostly I fished by feel.

Another cast, a sullen heaviness on the rod, and I was hooked up. A big walleye on a light rod is altogether different from a deep-water fish caught with clumsy gear and heavy sinkers. This one ran strongly out across the shoal, the drag of the reel whining in the dark.

Soon the fish was close, scraping against the canoe. I was fearful of the treble hooks, but a light could scare the others off the flat and end the fishing. I felt for the dorsal fin, reached just ahead of it, grasped the walleye behind the gill covers, and lifted it dripping into the canoe. It was a big female, much too big to take home. I managed to clear the hooks without the light, held the fish next to the canoe and felt it slide away as silently as it had come.

I cast again, hoping the school was still close in, but there was no stealthy pull this time, nor on the next several casts. I decided to wait, hoping another school would move onto the shoal. The night sounds crept closer again, and I heard a sudden snort and a crashing of brush—a deer had caught my scent on a vagary of wind and plunged back into the forest.

Waiting soundlessly in ambush in the canoe seemed in keeping with the feel of the night. Unlike largemouth bass, which feed aggressively after dark and don't care who knows it, the walleyes were silent as the mist when they came into shallow water. Only the skitter of a frightened baitfish might suggest their presence.

I cast again and hooked up immediately—a smaller walleye, about a pound and a half—and I slid it into a gunnysack. A fish thrashing and twisting on a stringer would surely frighten the others. Another cast brought a strike from an identical fish, but this one thumped against the canoe several times, rattling the lure against the metal, and I struggled to unhook it before the noise spooked the others.

But the next several casts were empty, and I knew the second school had vanished as silently as they had come. I felt suddenly stiff and more sore and realized I had been sitting for two hours in the same hunched position. Across the water a nestling loon wailed, and another answered close to the island.

I lifted the anchor and pushed off into the dark. It was a long pull, and once the canoe hit a rock and rang like an Oriental gong. Crossing open water, I paddled through a small flock of black ducks, gabbling softly and showing no fear of the canoe as they scrambled in a race to snap up spent mayflies spread-eagled on the water.

Back at the truck there was no need for silence, but still I tried to move quietly as I stowed my gear and heaved the canoe onto the rack, wincing as the metal gunwales grated the crossbeams.

With the canoe tied down, I walked back to the landing for a last look around. The lake was silent now, waiting for me to go.

Dark of Night

They say an angler goes through different stages, from wanting to catch any fish, to a lot of fish, to really big fish and finally to difficult fish. Maybe so, but even though I spend some time with the difficult fish, I confess that I still like to catch a big fish now and then.

The last time I felt this urge, after three days of not catching some difficult brown trout, I went to a deep, hard-fished pool, just off the main road. Many booted feet had tramped the short trail to this spot, and a few forked sticks stuck in the bank were proof that plenty of nightcrawlers had been soaked on the bottom.

For all the traffic, this was big fish water—deep, plenty of cover, lots of minnows. There was a riffle just downstream, crossed by a few strands of barbed wire, and below that a crumbling concrete bridge. Once, on the way back from an earlier evening's fishing I heard a heavy splash there. Climbing onto the bridge, I shined my flashlight into the water and saw a large brown trout holding in the current.

I was surprised to see the trout hold for at least a minute in the full glare of the light before it moved slowly upstream into the pool. Perhaps it was used to lights, since the broken beer bottles and other party favors suggested that the bridge was a favorite place for other kinds of nighttime recreation. I made a note to visit this place again.

The next time I arrived just before dark, rigged up with a 2X leader and a big Muddler Minnow, and eased into the stream just above the tailout, where I could cast a short line and swing the fly across the current. I made a few casts to get the distance right, stripped in the fly line, and held the loops of slack in my hand. Then I stood still and waited for darkness.

During the northern summer, darkness comes late. I saw a few dimples in the pool above, and I had to steel myself against the temptation to move up and cast to them. It was easy to imagine that a hatch was going on and the big trout had found something more interesting upstream, but I knew a three-or-four pound brown was not likely to be sipping little bugs when there were fat chubs and shiners to be had at night. Besides, any movement would send alarming ripples across the pool. So I waited.

The stars were out and the overhanging trees were silhouetted against them when I heard something large approaching through the woods. There was a splash, then another, and another. Then I heard a snort and the sound of something wading into the riffle. Fumbling in my bag, I snapped on the flashlight. Its beam caught the glowing eyes and the black and white face of a Holstein cow.

The cow didn't like the light and backed out of the water. The beam picked up the glow of other eyes back in the woods, and they too began to move off. At least they stayed on their side of the creek, but they made a lot of noise as they pushed through the undergrowth.

I thought the night was shot, but I decided to stay and wait just a bit longer. The light had nearly blinded me, and several long minutes passed before I could see in the dark again. Then I heard another splash, and this one sounded right—a big trout chasing a minnow in the shallows.

Preparing to cast, I found my fingers had stiffened while holding the slack, but I managed to work out the short line and cast across and downstream. The big Muddler dragged on the surface, and I could just make out its V-wake as it swung above the tailout. Nothing took hold, so I cast again, then waited several minutes more, listening for another splash.

I heard nothing, but I cast the big fly again, dragging it across the current. I was about to pick up when I felt a pluck. I was expecting a heavy pull, not a little bump, so I didn't react in time. I told myself it wasn't a rock—the pool was too deep to touch bottom without a heavily weighted fly and a sinking line.

Whatever it was, I decided to wait again and listen. This time I didn't have to wait long, for another heavy splash echoed from the far bank. I cast across, upstream from where I thought the splash was, and followed the fly around with the rod tip. I couldn't see the fly this time except in my mind's eye, because it had sunk below the surface. Still, I convinced myself that I could almost see it, or pretended that I could, much as I often did in daylight.

Halfway across the tailout, just as the line was coming tight in the current, I felt the little pluck again, and this time I struck back. The rod tip yanked sharply down and the reel screeched as the big trout bolted, thrashing its way through the tailout, over the shallow gravel shoal, and down into the blackness beneath the bridge. Then I remembered the strands of barbed wire stretched across the riffle.

Keeping the rod tip as low as I could, I stumbled into the tailout and down toward the wire, trying to imagine how I would pass the rod under the fence and climb over it. I couldn't see the wire, so I ran downstream in a low crouch like a Walter Mitty fullback, forearm extended, until I collided with the fence.

The reel was still running, so I pushed the rod under the water, let go, and scrambled over the fence gambling that I could find the rod again. I knew it was a big fish, but you don't think about the price of a rod and reel at a time like this. As I cleared the wire, ever the picture of grace, I grabbed for my flashlight and caught the silver gleam of the reel as it bumped along the rocky bottom. I reached deep and snatched up the rod in triumph.

But there was no heavy throbbing—nothing but the drag of the line in the current. I reeled up quickly, hoping the trout had turned upstream, but then I felt the leader knots clicking through the guides, and there was no Muddler on the tippet. Cold water began to creep into my waders, and I knew I hadn't quite cleared the barbed-wire fence after all.

Well, at least I know where to go if that big fish urge strikes again. In the meantime, I think I'll give some of those difficult fish another try.

III

Luck

Close Call

It began innocently enough. I knew the river fairly well—enough to carry a stout wading staff—and I had recently replaced the felt soles on my wading shoes. So when I saw a good fish rise across a heavy current strewn with big boulders, I was confident I could wade to the right position, make the right cast, and pick him off—a textbook case.

The water was deep between the boulders, but though it was still early, the morning light was bright enough to see the bottom. The water had an amber tint from the northern forest bogs, like weak tea, but over the years I had learned to read such water fairly well—better, perhaps, than the transparent clarity of mountain streams out west. My wife was still asleep in the tent, and a family camped further upstream was just beginning to stir. I could see a wisp of smoke rising from their fire ring and a little girl swinging her red and yellow teddy bear by the arm. With a cloudless blue sky overhead, I knew the river would soon be fully exposed to the sunlight, and the trout now rising so steadily would likely move to the shadows.

Downstream, the river narrowed into a churning whitewater rapids, the foamy spray sparkling in the early sun. It was a real canoe-killer. A line of haystack waves marched right down the middle, and several sweepers trailed their broken branches in the bluster of the current. Looking again at the boulders and the friendlier water upstream, I planned my route. With careful wading I could take advantage of the slack water behind the big rock. There was only one place that looked difficult, but if I could get close enough, I could cast across, mend upstream, and still get a good drift. A big fish rose again, and that settled it.

I stepped into the water and what I had come to call the "Joe Brooks two-step." Joe Brooks had written about wading heavy water with a staff, advising his readers to plant the staff firmly first, then take two careful steps, plant the staff again, take two more steps, and so on, so you would always have two points of contact with the bottom. It worked well, even on the slick round boulders of the Madison River below Yellowstone Park. They used to say the wardens came through weekly to grease the rocks near Slide Inn. Compared to that stuff, this looked easy.

I made it to the backwash behind the first big boulder. I had seen no rises in that spot, but it looked good, so I drifted a fly through the tongue of current a few times, then picked up and began to cast over and across again toward the rising fish I really wanted. The current was strong and nearly hip deep, and I was further downstream than I wanted to be, but I pushed across again, focused and confident with my staff and felt soles, staying with the Joe Brooks two-step, not getting careless.

Then, in what seemed like just another step forward, the bottom gravel began to roll out from under my wading shoes. Instinctively I stepped back, and the planted foot began to slip as well. I was suddenly afraid. The wading staff was still firmly stuck in the bottom. It was a sturdy fiberglass stick, but now it was wobbling against the force of the current and the downward pressure of my hand.

It was like standing on a hill of marbles. I could feel the bottom gravel creeping out from under me. The rapids downstream, its churning and bubbling once cheerful in the early morning light, now sounded much louder and more threatening. I knew I was in big trouble, and I felt the rush of fear and adrenaline wash over me.

"Jude!" I called to my wife. "Jude, I need help! Now!" Odd how calling to her for help seemed less embarrassing than calling to total strangers in plain view. Meanwhile, as I tried again to shift my footing, the gravel rolled alarmingly, and I lifted my staff and stabbed for the bottom. It held for the moment, but I knew it was only temporary.

Looking upstream, I called again for help. I saw my wife's head emerge from the tent, and beyond her, at the next campsite, I saw a teen-aged boy look right at me, wide-eyed, then turn in a moment of decision and reach for an axe. With two strokes he had cut their clothesline and in a single movement he stripped the brightly colored T-shirts, jeans, and socks from it. Then he began to run toward me. He was running fast, clawing his way through the brush, but he looked very far away.

The bottom gravel shifted again, tearing my glance away from the boy. I knew if I didn't make a strong move I would slip again, and maybe this time nothing would hold me. The rapids downstream sounded even louder, and the haystacks seemed to dash against each other with great fury.

Greatly daring, I took a long stride backward, pivoted downstream to face the bank, and swung my staff for new purchase on the bottom. Nothing rolled out from under me, and I strode along again as soon as the staff was planted. That was enough, and the bottom was suddenly as firm as a sidewalk. A few steps more and I was in thigh-deep water, breathing hard, but safe.

Leaning heavily against my staff and looking up, I saw the boy slowing to a stop, the clothesline trailing behind him, and my wife, her hair tousled from sleep, standing next to our little tent, a hand to her mouth. Further in the background, caught in the swirl of smoke from their campfire, I saw the boy's parents and his little sister, still clutching her teddy bear, all frozen like a photograph.

"I'm O.K., thanks—thanks a lot," I said to the boy, then louder to the others, "I'm O.K.!"

Across the river the trout rose again.

Dumb Luck

A friend from the university brought his young son north to visit us at our old log cabin on Lake Superior. The boy had insisted he wanted to learn to cast a fly, and they had come up so that I could teach him—probably because I was the only fly fisherman he knew. Certainly it wasn't for my renown as a fly-caster.

The boy had sent me flies of his own design since he turned five (they were very colorful, to say the least), and now that he was ten, he wanted to learn to cast and really start catching fish. He had saved up and bought a fly outfit, and though everything was still brand-new and untried, it had been lovingly handled. The reel's cardboard box had been opened and closed many times and was already wrinkled. All through lunch he asked about the fishing nearby, what flies I thought were best, when I planned to go fishing again, what knots I used, what my favorite fish was, and so on, and he told us all about fishing near his home.

The boy's disappointment was keen when I took him to the little cemetery near our cabin instead of a secret trout stream for our casting lesson, but I explained it was best to learn to cast here, where there were no fish to distract us. After sawing the air back and forth for a half hour or so, he started to get the idea—at least enough so he could practice on his own—and I had escaped permanent damage.

At the beginning of the lesson, he wanted me to show him how far I could cast. Like many beginning fly fishermen, he thought casting far was more important the casting accurately. So I said, "I'd rather show you how I cast when I'm fishing." I dropped my hat on the ground, walked about 20 feet away, crouched low on one knee, began to cast the hookless fly to the hat, and actually hit it several times—but not enough to make much of an impression. He still wanted to know how far I could cast.

Since there was still time in the afternoon before they had to leave for home, his father asked if I would take them to a spot along the shore where they could cast for lake trout. I agreed, and before long, after a ten-minute drive and a short tramp through the woods, we emerged on a rocky point splashed with bright orange lichens and lapped by clear swells. It felt as if the lake were slowly breathing in the calm of the afternoon.

There is a heavily traveled path to that point now, and it is commonplace to see three or four people beating the water in late summer, but to me it was known as "Ingram's Rock," a name I gave it for the many hours I had fished there with my old neighbor. I think he liked to fish with me because, although he was deaf, he could still hear me without his hearing aid. When fishing was slow, he would tell me the old stories about the CCC camps, deer hunting, forest fires, and of course, fishing. I had heard them before, many times, but it was good to see the light in the old man's eyes as he recounted his adventures.

I tried to suggest something of this to the boy and his father as we clambered over the glacier-polished rock to the end of the point, but they were eager to fish, and after all, there really wasn't anything special about this particular rock. I was probably the only one who paid any attention to the blue harebells nodding from their niches in the basalt.

As I helped the boy assemble his spinning outfit, his father took charge and began to cast a spoon. Before I could offer any suggestions, he promptly hung up his first cast and had to break off. Picking up my own spinning rod, I said, "You don't want to cast to the light-colored areas. It's too shallow there. You might want to cast over here." And with that I made a cast to the deeper water, just to show him.

As luck would have it, I got a heavy pull, and after several dogged runs and some scrambling among the slippery rocks I had a pale and glistening 12-pound lake trout in the landing net—the biggest I had ever caught in that spot. The boy's eyes were round with wonder, as if the Wizard of Oz had suddenly appeared before him. To make matters worse, no other fish took hold, even though the boy and his father cast diligently for the next two hours.

As they cast, the boy kept asking me about the trout, now tucked away in a damp gunnysack. Every now and then he would stop casting, open the bag and peek inside, and then he would ask again to show him exactly where I had cast, how fast I retrieved the orange and silver spoon, what test my line was, etc., etc.

I tried to explain that catching the big trout was just luck. There was nothing special about my rod, reel, line, lure, or casting skill. True, I had known enough to cast to the deeper water, the hooks had been carefully sharpened, and I did manage to land the fish on a fairly light outfit. But he was convinced that he was in the presence of genius, which was flattering in its way, and he insisted that I show him my secret.

Finally I said, "Look, I really don't have any secrets. It was just dumb luck that the trout happened to swim along here just as I cast."

As boys often do, he scuffed his toe at the lichens and looked down at his own spinning outfit, untouched by magic. "Maybe it was dumb luck to you," he said, "but it looked like smart luck to me."

One-Cast Wonders

On a sunny April morning my wife and I decided to drive up the Door Peninsula, visit Bailey's Harbor, Cave Point, and a few other pleasant spots, and have dinner somewhere on the way back.

A few hours later, as we rolled along a narrow cedar-lined road, we came to a culvert where a small stream paused once more before flowing into Lake Michigan. There was a good current through the pool below the culvert, and two anglers stood in the tailout.

Fishing water never looks more promising than when you must pass it by, but this was the third or fourth stream we had crossed, and I couldn't drive on without stopping for at least a minute or two. My wife sighed resignedly as we pulled off onto the roadside. She sighed again, a bit more menacingly this time, when I reached behind the front seat and pulled out a rod case.

In a felt hat, tie, and tweed sportcoat, I was dressed for an altogether different occasion, but I put the fly rod together, attached the reel, and tied on an orange and white steelhead fly. "I'll just try a couple of casts near the culvert," I said reassuringly, but my wife had already settled in for a siege and opened a thick paperback novel.

Realizing I was on thin ice, I walked quickly to the tail of the pool and asked the two anglers if I could make a few casts up near the culvert. One of them looked me up and down, as if sizing up the threat I posed to their fishing, but finally said, "Sure, go ahead."

I walked back up to the road and stepped down into the matted brown grass next to the culvert. I planned to cast across the main current and let the fly come around in a classic wet-fly swing. The fly was tied on a heavy-wire hook, and the sink-tip line would take it down.

The two anglers exchanged amused smiles as the tweedy figure above them moved cautiously into position, but they said nothing. One of them retrieved his spawn bag and sent a long cast arching up near the culvert's mouth, drifting the bait down into the slower water.

All too mindful of my audience, I stripped line off the reel, false-cast four or five times, laid out the fly across and slightly downstream, then flipped a mend upstream. The fly barely had begun its swing when the line was yanked tight and five pounds of silver steelhead burst through the surface.

Trying not to get my shoes wet, I walked around through the dead grass to the tailout, following the run downstream. A few minutes later the fish was thrashing almost at the feet of the two anglers, who reeled up and backed out of the stream to give me room. They were popeyed with surprise as I beached the steelhead and pulled out the brightly colored fly, which was stuck firmly in the corner of its mouth. They shook their heads and muttered something I couldn't quite hear, but it sounded prayerful.

"Thanks, fellas," I said as I reeled up, clipped off the fly, and stowed the rod in the car. As I opened the door, my wife looked up from her book.

"Back so soon?" she asked, a tinge of irony in her voice.

"Sometimes one cast is all it takes," I said, holding up the fish.

After sliding the fish into a plastic bag and taking down the rod, I glanced back at the two anglers. They had both waded back into the tailout and were obviously still discussing what they had witnessed. As I got back behind the wheel and started the engine, one lifted a hand in salute, and I waved back—not too jauntily, I hope.

As we drove away, I told my wife that these one-cast wonders had happened before, and not just to me. I recalled an instance the previous fall, when a number of us were standing on a pier casting spoons for rainbows. It seemed we had the fish outnumbered at least ten to one, but a few had been caught—enough to keep us hopeful.

A tourist in a yellow sportshirt, glossy white shoes and lime-green pants wandered out on the pier, looked admiringly at the big rainbows on stringers here and there, and walked purposefully back to town. Soon he returned with a brand-new spincast outfit. A blue and silver spoon dangled from the rod tip, tied to the fluorescent blue monofilament with a large but uncertain-looking knot.

He picked an open spot, stood at the edge of the concrete, and flung out a high-arching cast that splashed down a few yards out. As luck would have it, a rainbow of about nine pounds took a liking to his spoon among all the others just like it, and suddenly his new reel was screeching as the trout surged away.

Frantic advice came from all sides, but he was deaf to it. Hunching over, he pointed the five-foot rod straight at the fish and began to reel. Someone shouted at him to pump the fish in, dramatically pantomiming the motions, but he had eyes only for his fish and continued to crank the protesting reel against the drag.

Some rainbow trout are street-smart delinquents, and this was one of them. Instead of racing further away, it suddenly turned and ran straight at its tormentor. The tourist cranked faster as the fish rushed toward him, but he couldn't keep up. The twisted line went slack, and I heard a "Whfft!" as it spun itself around the rod tip.

After running almost to his feet, the rainbow bolted straight away. The coils of slack straightened, and there was a frozen moment. The blue monofilament whined with the strain, then popped like a pistol shot. The tourist tottered, lost his balance, and fell face first into the water. We had to use a long-handled net to pull him along the algae-slicked pier to shore. He was still clutching his rod when we hauled him out—pale, shivering, oblivious to the poorly-hidden laughter swirling around him, convinced the trout had jerked him bodily into the lake.

Sometimes one cast is all it takes.

Osprey Luck

I think nearly every fisherman is secretly attentive to matters of luck. Even those of recent vintage, the neophytes from the weekend fly-fishing schools, soon discovered that certain objects or events—a sweat-stained hat, an unusual flower, an obscure brand of smoking tobacco, the call of a tundra swan, a shooting star at sunset—can be mysteriously conjoined with the chances of taking a good fish.

Years ago, luck was a frequent theme in the literature of angling. Henry Van Dyke, a Princeton theologian, wrote a delightfully nostalgic book unapologetically entitled *Fisherman's Luck*, and in his classic *Upstream and Down* Howard T. Walden said that chancing upon a trillium would bring good luck—and that catching a trout on the first cast was the worst luck, dooming the angler to a fishless day. Now, as techno-babble fills modern fishing books and magazines, luck is rarely mentioned, but there remains in fishing an elemental feeling for omens and portents, as it must have been when prehistoric fishermen in dugout canoes dropped bone hooks into the deep and carved totems to lure fish and ward off sea monsters.

Signs and omens of fishing luck are highly personal. What may be of cosmic significance for an angler is background noise or the worst sort of bad luck for another. With some trepidation I confess that, for me, seeing an osprey brings good luck, though just what shape "osprey luck" will take remains obscure.

I was first alerted to the luck brought by these kindred spirits while fishing a small trout lake near the Boundary Waters Canoe Area Wilderness. I should have been concentrating on retrieving my deeply sunk Muddler Minnow, but my glance was torn away by the splash of a osprey diving for a trout on shallow flat. Though not rare, ospreys are far from numerous in the clear, deep lakes of northeastern Minnesota. I watched as the osprey labored free of the water, beating its long wings and clutching a heavy trout in one foot, then transferring it to both feet with the head pointed forward—something only an osprey can do.

After several more casts I felt a pluck at the Muddler and set up on a strong fish. Backing that had never before seen the light of day spun off the reel and into the tannin-stained water. Far way, a silver scimitar sliced through the surface and fell back, and I knew I had an exceptional trout, if I could but get him in. Several long runs and a near disaster with the anchor rope later, a prime 23-inch rainbow trout lay gasping in my landing net. I clipped off the tippet rather than probe for the fly, turned the net inside out, and held the fish upright for several minutes until it finned away.

Some of us are slow to recognize the omens of good luck, even when they are obvious to the enlightened. A few weeks later another osprey sighting led to a fine catch of smallmouth bass. The osprey cannonballed into the water several times without success, but I caught and released seven bass from two to nearly five pounds, all feeding on emerging *Hexagenia* mayflies in a shallow bay—an exceptional bag in a hard-fished lake where small-mouths grow slowly and trophy fish are rare.

It took a third revelation to confirm beyond doubt that ospreys portend good luck—this time a nesting pair. As I paddled along a steep, jackpine-crowned shoreline, I could see their ramshackle nest and hear the cries of their nestlings. Then I saw an adult osprey arrive with a fish. This was a cue for another adult to leave on a fishing expedition while the nestlings clambered about the nest, calling incessantly and flapping their newly fledged wings. The adults flew off and returned several times with fish for their impatient offspring—some enviable trout among them. As it grew dark, their foraging ceased, and a mayfly hatch began just as the light faded in the west.

Casting my dry fly toward the last of the afterglow, I was aware of night-hawks and brown bats fluttering overhead, dipping occasionally near the surface to scoop up an emerging mayfly. After a few moments, I twitched the fly, trying to suggest a bit of life struggling to free itself from the surface film. Instantly a bat swooped down and picked it up. Flying in a widening spiral above my head, the bat lifted my fly line off the water. I stripped in slowly, wondering what to do, while the bat fluttered unseen over my head. When the leader knots began to click through the guides I pointed the rod toward the west, silhouetting the bat against the fading light. I could just make out the fly stuck at the very tip of the bat's lower jaw. I began to swing it back and forth like a pendulum. After a few swings, I snapped the rod tip back, hoping to break the leader. Instead, the fly popped out intact, the bat fluttered wildly for a second and went on its way.

Undaunted by this most unusual event, I made another cast and promptly hooked up on a solid rainbow that ran well into the backing and made several crashing jumps in the enfolding dark. With the aid of a flashlight I measured the fish at just under 20 inches—a very good one for that lake, and final confirmation that, for me at least, an osprey sighting meant good luck. The truth now revealed, I could recall other occasions where good luck had come with ospreys—and that led to unshakable conviction. As with the newly converted everywhere, I marveled at my own insensitivity in failing to recognize the importance of osprey luck in my earlier fishing career, that big northern pike we caught in Pickerel Narrows, for example, or a stringer of fat bluegills from a Michigan pond, or my first five-pound brook trout in Lake Nipigon.

Years later, fishing with Captain Rob Fordyce in the Everglades, I saw several ospreys during our third morning's fishing and incautiously announced that we would have good luck. In response to his puzzled look, I took a big chance and explained the phenomenon of osprey luck in some detail, well aware that revealing the portents of good luck could cause an imp from the nether regions to pop out and tangle my backcast at a crucial moment. But I was careful to note with proper humility that osprey luck didn't always come the same day. It could take a day or two, possibly more, but we were sure to have good luck before the week was out.

On our fifth and last day of fishing, we left the dock at Flamingo and motored up the Buttonwood Channel in a straight-down south Florida rain. I had to admit, somewhat fearfully, that osprey luck had not yet manifested itself. We had caught several snook and redfish early in the week and released a whopping 115-pound tarpon the day before I saw the ospreys. But boating the big tarpon didn't count as osprey luck—it never comes before a sighting, always afterward. Rob tried to dodge from storm to storm, but the rain came down so hard we were forced to hole up in a chickee, to the delight of local mosquitoes. I saw that osprey luck would be sorely tested in this deluge.

Finally the rain relented enough for us to leave the chickee, but sky and water were iron gray as we swiftly ran the skiff toward a promising bay, very near where we had seen the ospreys. Wet and pocked with mosquito bites, I began to wonder if my osprey luck had finally run out, but as we emerged from a narrow channel, we saw what must have been at least a hundred tarpon rolling. "When they come in like that, they're here to eat," said Rob. "We're going to be busy."

The calm surface was like a steel plate, broken occasionally by a fin or a rolling fish. Three times I cast to a tarpon, only to drop the fly line over an unseen companion that bolted away, spooking its neighbors. Finally a tarpon rolled 40 feet out, showing enough direction to enable me to place the cast well and quickly. Stripping slowly, I felt the fly stop and set the hook in a 100-pounder that responded by hurling itself through the surface, thrashing and rattling as if it were about to fly apart. Eleven desperate jumps later, the tarpon settled into a steady, unrelenting pull, sheer muscle against my straining 10- weight fly rod.

Then, as Rob tried to get a better angle with the camera, he lost the pushpole overboard, and I had to fight the tarpon from a dead boat. I finally managed to get the fish close after two more jumps, but it took several minutes of lifting almost straight up before Rob could grasp its lower jaw.

Sweating in my rain gear throughout the battle, I was too tired to do more than lift the tarpon's head out of the water for a quick photograph. I had mistakenly laid my fly rod on the casting deck in front of me, and I didn't dare to try to lift the fish over it. Hurrying to revive the exhausted tarpon, Rob seized its tail, turned the fish gently into the current to oxygenate its gills, then shoved it forward beneath the polished surface, now strewn with patches of white foam from all the jumping and thrashing.

Recovering slowly from the excitement (and from 45 minutes of heavy lifting), I stripped off my sodden rain gear and drank almost a quart of water as Rob tied on a new leader and fly, then started the motor and idled over to retrieve his pushpole. The sound of the motor would likely put the fish down, but as he picked up the pole and shut down the motor, a light breeze came up, not quite enough to ripple the surface. Here and there a tarpon showed silver against the calm. In a few more minutes the tarpon seemed to return, though we saw fewer fins and breaks than before, and we knew they were nervous now.

As the sky brightened behind us, another tarpon rolled about 100 feet away, flashing silver, then another still further out. A flock of ibis flew overhead, brilliant white and black against the dark, gray water, and landed in the tops of the mangrove trees. I turned to Rob and said, "You know, it's perfect right now. Maybe we should just leave them and remember it like this."

But Rob's good judgment prevailed over my romantic impulses, and the skiff began to move as the moist wind picked it up a bit. "There are tarpon all around us," he whispered. "Let's just drift through them and cast." Silently he placed the pushpole in the chocks, reached under the gunwale, and pulled out a 12-weight fly rod with a slow-sinking line and an orange and red "shark dredger" fly. We both began to cast as the wind gently nudged the skiff toward the tarpon.

A few minutes later, as I turned to say something to Rob, his rod hand jerked violently back, and a huge tarpon rolled heavily off the stern. A powerful wake surged toward the skiff as Rob frantically stripped line, trying to come tight to the fish. A few feet from the stern, the tarpon burst through the surface, coming right at Rob, its mouth wide open and I thought he would be knocked from the deck like a bowling pin. His rod was pointed straight at the fish, and I saw the tip recoil as the tarpon brushed against it, caromed off the motor, and crashed down onto the pushpole. The pole shattered right at the gunwale, and after two more jumps the tarpon was off.

I stood open-mouthed on the casting deck, my fly line trailing forgotten in the dark water. When my voice returned, I asked, "How big was he, Rob?"

"At least a hundred and forty," he said, shaking his head, then added the obvious in his soft south Florida accent, "He broke mah pushpole!"

How could I ever again doubt osprey luck after such a day?

The Breakoff

I arrived later than I intended at a small trout lake. The morning sun was well up and it was already getting too warm. Several small boats were anchored along the shoals, and as I lugged my float tube to the water's edge, one boat was coming back in. An elderly man and his young grandson pulled in at the landing.

I greeted them in the usual fashion—"Any luck?"—not really expecting any information, but the boy was obviously excited about something. I held the bow of the boat steady while his grandfather climbed out, and together we pulled it up on shore.

"Well, we broke off a real nice one," he said as he began to pull apart the sections of an old glass fly rod. "Just couldn't hold'im."

The boy chimed, "Yeah! Grandpa said it musta been a three-pounder at least! We saw it jump!" He looked up admiringly at this grandfather, the way I suppose all grandparents would like to be looked at by the grandchildren.

The old man might not have wanted to say much more, but with his grandson there, I suppose he couldn't resist. He explained how they had hit the water at sunup, hoping there would be a hatch. They caught a few small rainbows, he said, but when nothing much emerged, they began to drift and troll with a wet fly.

"A Grizzly King," the boy prompted. The boy had a lot to learn about keeping secrets. I admitted I would not have expected that old pattern to be the hot fly.

"Yep," said the old man. "He hit real hard, jumped a couple of times, and then just took off and never stopped." He smiled down at this grandson. "Well, we better get goin', boy. Your ma will have lunch ready at the campground."

I asked if they were staying at the campground where I intended to set up for a couple of days, and the boy said they were. He started to ask about my float tube, but his grandfather interrupted and said they had to leave. I helped him slide his boat into the back of his pickup truck, and then they were gone.

I felt good about the conversation. The boy was getting off to a good start and was excited about this grandfather's success, even if they had lost a big fish. Besides, aren't those the ones we remember best?

Most of the boats on the lake were anchored in the best spots, so I pumped up my float tube and began fishing in my usual fashion by prospecting with a sinking fly line and a big nymph. The sun was bright overhead, and I knew business wouldn't pick up until later, but it was fun to be out and doing.

The afternoon passed lazily, and business did indeed begin to pick up as the sun neared the treeline. I released several small rainbows, then finned my way in and anchored the tube quietly near a weedy shoal—a good place for an evening rise. I rerigged with a floating fly line, an extra-long leader, and a small olive-brown hare's ear nymph.

Two solid fish took the nymph in the next hour, both about 15 inches, and I kept one for the grill. I also released a few more small ones. As evening came on, I greased the leader to hold the nymph higher, expecting the trout to start cruising nearer the surface.

A few minutes later I hooked up, and a strong fish surged away into the deep water. It was the biggest fish of the day, about 17 inches, and as I netted it I saw a bright green and gray fly stuck in its nose—a home-tied Grizzly King. A few inches of the broken leader were still attached, along with a couple of wind knots.

As the trout lay in the net, I puzzled about what to do. I could kill the fish and bring it to the campground with the fly intact. That would be a great story for the boy to tell his friends. On the other hand, while it was a nice trout, it wasn't anywhere near three pounds, so that might not be so good. Or I could just say nothing about it.

More on impulse that anything, I reached down with the forceps, popped out the Grizzly King, then removed my small nymph and tipped the trout out of the net. It swam off strongly despite its travails, and I began to find my way back to the landing.

After stowing my gear in the pickup, I drove to the campground. In the glow of a campfire I saw the boy, his grandfather, and the rest of the family sitting around toasting marshmallows. I still wasn't sure what I would say, but I stopped and walked over with the Grizzly King.

"Recognize this fly?" I asked, holding it out in the firelight. The old man and boy came over, peered in my hand, and looked up, astonished.

"Where'd you get that fly?" they asked in unison, but of course they knew the answer. I explained that I caught their trout in the early evening and had decided to release it, since I already had a fish in my bag.

"Besides, a trout that big needs to go back," I said, handing the fly to the boy. "I guess there's still magic in that old Grizzly King."

The boy looked up at his grandfather proudly. "Grandpa is a real good fisherman," he said. "He even ties his own flies." Then he ran off to show the others. The old man began to follow, then he turned back to me.

"How big was that fish?" he asked—the question I had wanted to avoid, but I knew I couldn't.

"Oh, I'd say right around three pounds," I replied, spreading my hands. "Biggest I've seen in quite a while."

He smiled, nodded firmly, and turned again to follow his grandson back to the campfire.

Well—what would *you* have said?

IV

Trout

Beaver Pond

The faint sun rose weakly through the mists that overhung the beaver pond. The dead aspen and spruce trees leaned at odd angles, their bare branches seeming to grope through the morning fog. I was making a similar gesture, trying to see more clearly.

I had packed in over a difficult trail the afternoon before and set up camp on a dry hump surrounded by swamp ooze, dead spruce and tag alders. Arriving just before dark, I had no time to try the pond. I threw the tent up, gathered some dry beaver sticks from the dam for firewood, and got organized.

The mosquitoes had long since discovered me, and along with a few spruce needles and other flotsam in the pot, they probably added something to the flavor of my morning tea. Everything was damp, and the crackling of the campfire seemed very loud in the silence of the dawn.

Beaver ponds have always been a problem for me. I have seen good trout streams go bad when a new beaver dam slowed the flow and warmed the water. But I think this pond must have had several springs that kept it cool, and it had been a steady producer of handsome, dark-backed brook trout for several years. Its black water always had an element of mystery. Despite its remoteness, it was far from a sure thing, and I had been skunked there before, especially on bright, sunny days.

As the mists hung over the water, the pond looked like polished metal, and nothing disturbed the surface. I sat and drank my tea and waited for the fog to lift. I heard a pileated woodpecker call and begin to excavate a dead snag near the dam. Moved by this example of industry, I threw the rest of the tea into the fire and began to assemble my tackle. The plan was to fish early, before the sun put the fish down. That was why I packed in the day before. Hurrying a little now, I put out the fire and pushed through the alders toward the dam.

I came out at the stream just below the dam and noticed some freshly peeled sticks in among the older ones. The pond was still a "live" pond, and I saw where the beavers had gone far back in the woods to gnaw down aspen and drag them to the water. As long as they could find food, they would keep the dam in good repair.

Staying low, I crept closer, knowing the trout often held in the deep water just above the dam. Almost imperceptibly the mists began to disappear. I tied on a Pass Lake wet fly, straightened the leader tippet, and moved up a few more feet.

The sun came through the fog just a I made my first cast—enough so I could see several dark shapes with white-edged fins rising swiftly through the water. The fly was taken before it had the chance to sink, and I was hooked fast in the first trout of the day, a plump 13-incher. I could see another trout darting in and out, trying to take away the fly.

The others disappeared when the hooked trout broke the surface, and a few moments later I had him in hand, moist and beautiful in the early morning light. I was tempted—a meal of fresh trout in that lonely spot would be hard to beat—but I decided he was too big for the pan and slid him back. A couple of 9-inchers would be more suitable. Besides, there were more trout to be had.

Or so I thought. But seeing is one thing, catching another, even back in the puckerbrush. The other trout near the dam had spooked, and the Pass Lake fly went through several casts untouched. I changed to a small black Woolly Bugger, thinking a leech-like fly worked along the bottom would be irresistible, but except for one light tap, nothing took hold

It's hard to leave a spot when you know fish are there, but I finally began to work my way up one side of the pond. "Work" is right: it took me almost an hour of floundering to find my way to go to a log where I could stand and cast, and on the way I stepped into a beaver hole, snagged my shirt on a sharp stub, and fell several times.

The log sagged further into the water when I stepped on it, stirring up a cloud of muck—a warning that the bottom was soft. But undaunted, I changed back to the Pass Lake fly, edged out a little further, and cast, just missing the dead trees behind me.

The fly sank slowly into the dark water, and I had just lost sight of it when the leader snapped straight. I wasn't quite prepared for such a pull. As the slack jumped out of my fingers, I glanced down to clear it. That was a mistake. I overbalanced, reached out to steady myself, and then the log and I parted company.

I suppose it's an angler's instinct to keep the rod tip up when he falls in, so I probably resembled the Statue of Liberty when I hit the water. But, mindful of the soft bottom, I caught hold of the log with my left arm and managed to straddle it. I am not a horseman, but I clung to that log like a rodeo bronco and brought the trout in, a near twin of the first.

"You I will eat," I said. There was no need to dampen my fish bag for its newest occupant. I sloshed back to my campsite, rather less heedful of the muck and the holes. Soon the surrounding limbs were decorated with my shirt, pants, hip boots, and socks, and I was grateful for the comfort of dry clothes.

I pulled another campfire together, set up my fire grate, and soon had two orange brook trout fillets sputtering in the pan, along with a can of baked beans and a pot of hot water for tea—with a few more mosquitoes and spruce needles for seasoning.

Itty-Bitties

Crouched below a slow-moving pool on a spring creek in southwest Wisconsin's driftless area, I watched several trout rising busily, but I couldn't make out what they were taking. It was hot, well past the prime time for the larger mayflies, and the rises were small and subtle—not splashy enough for caddis.

Since these were the first active fish I had seen in a slow morning, I decided to find out what they were taking, rather than just tossing something out and hoping to pick off the village idiot.

I knelt and crept close to the tailout as I could without sending a warning ripple upstream. With my nose close to the water, I could make out a parade of tiny mayflies. Dipping one out with my aquarium net, I could see it plainly for the first time—pale cream abdomen, dark thorax, and tiny grey wings.

I retreated to the bank and dug out my "micro" fly box, hoping to find something similar. Previous disappointments had taught me the folly of casting a standard-size dry fly at trout that were feeding on such small stuff. Besides, I wanted to see if I could get close enough to the real thing.

The little mayfly was tangled in the wet meshes of the net, so I could try several flies on for size, so to speak. A #16 dry fly placed next to the tiny fly looked huge, and even a #20 was too big. I finally found a #20 that had more or less the right color and trimmed it back a little with a scissors.

After tying it on a long 7X tippet, I crawled back to a good casting position, made a measuring cast off to one side, and then cast just above the closest riser. The fish could see the leader as well as the fly. The naturals were smaller than some of the leader knots, but I hoped the flexibility of the fine monofilament and a natural drift would "sell" the fly and draw a rise.

I couldn't really see the fly on the water, but my measuring cast told me about where it was as it drifted downstream. Everything worked out at planned, and I released two decent brown trout before the others were put down. A 7X tippet is surprisingly strong, and I was able to pull both fish downstream away from the others and into the riffle. But there was still too much commotion. The dainty rises stopped and the pool became quiet.

I waited, hoping the trout would resume feeding, but finally I gave up and began to move upstream. I was congratulating myself on this small triumph when I turned the corner and met another angler sitting on the bank with half a dozen fly boxes open and spread before him. I started to make a wide circle around him, but he looked up as I approached.

"Do any good?" he asked.

"Well, not much," I replied, "I did get a couple in that last pool. You do anything?"

He replied that he had not had a strike all morning. The lamb's-wool patch on his vest was covered with flies, wet and dry, all tried and found wanting.

"I saw a few rises," he said, "but I couldn't get 'em to hit. What were you using?"

I thought to myself how typical our little dialogue was—and how often I had been the one not to catch anything. I also knew that some anglers made a very big deal out of catching a trout on a very small fly, as if it required something special in the way of skill or talent.

I told him about the hatch of little mayflies and the small dry fly. Then I showed him the fly, still tied to the end of the leader.

He snorted in disbelief as he peered at it. "You actually caught somethin' on that itty-bitty thing?"

I had to smile at his use of a term I hadn't heard since childhood, but I assured him that a couple of fish did move to it.

"Couldn't have been very big," he said with conviction. "Myself, I like to give the fish somethin' to eat." I had to admit that I also preferred that approach, but there did seem to be times when only a small fly would work, especially in tailwaters and clear spring creeks.

I left him then, still contemplating his open fly boxes, and moved back away from the stream. I sensed that he had already written me off as a fly-fishing snob for even daring to show him a #20 fly.

I could understand. When I fished for trout with worms and spinners, the few fly fishermen I met seemed to think I was a dim-witted clodhopper and a menace to the trout. As I learned to use flies, I caught a lot of fish and was actually more of a menace than I was with worms—perhaps even more so because of my self-satisfaction in ascending to a higher social rank.

Eventually I found there were just too many rungs on the fly-fishing ladder. Out west, in the Yellowstone country, if I caught trout on a House and Lot (a "dude fly"), somebody more expert caught them on a Pale Morning Dun. If I did well with a Pheasant Tail Emerger, someone else was using a Stillborn Dun fished in the film. I once spent several days infested by an angler who constantly referred to bugs but shortening their Latin names to "flavs" and "paraleps," but he quit talking to me when I asked him if he could show me how to fish Woolly Worms with a sinking line.

Nowadays, like the guy sitting on the bank of the spring creek, I try to give the fish "somethin' to eat," but it doesn't much matter what size the fly is or what it's called, as long as the fish like it.

Even if it's an "itty-bitty."

Pocket Water

After a long morning's fishing I found myself where I shouldn't have been on a bright, hot day—in the middle of a large sunstruck pool. There were no shady banks, no big rocks, just a stretch of clear, flat water where I could see every pebble on the bottom. My leader projected an intermittent shadow wherever I cast, even though I had scaled down to 7X and a small nymph, and no trout had shown any interest since shortly after sunup.

The discouraged looks of two other anglers near the head of the pool confirmed that they had done no better. They were both mumbling about early morning tricos and changing from one tiny fly to another, without result.

I got out of the river then and hiked half a mile upstream along the railroad grade. Well before I could see the river again, I could hear it tumbling around the boulders left by the last glacial ice. This was pocket water, full of little hidey-holes, some surprisingly deep, behind and between the rocks—cool, safe, and full of oxygen. And trout, or so I hoped.

I re-rigged with a 3X tippet and two #12 wet flies—a Coachman as the dropper and a Dark Cahill on the point, about 30 inches apart. Staying low and making short casts across and downstream, I moved from one pocket to another, never fishing more than two rod lengths of line. By reaching across the currents, I could swim the flies up into the back eddies, twitch them across the surface, or drop them down for a short drift before picking them up again.

Not every fish that came to the flies actually took hold, but several showed themselves, making what G.E.M. Skues called "that brown wink in the water" as they turned away. Each time a fish showed in a pocket, I worked the flies back through it again and again. If I didn't hook up, I mentally marked the spot for the return trip.

I was abruptly reminded that you need to plan ahead in pocket-water fishing when the first good fish I hooked shot out of the pocket, flashing bronze and yellow, ran downstream in the fast water, and broke me off in a jumble of driftwood. I should have anticipated that move and prepared myself to pressure the fish quickly across the sluice and into another pocket where I could have netted him.

Working further downstream, I hooked and released seven handsome brown trout, four of them big enough to know better. At the bottom of the rapids the current slowed and spread out into a long pool. After a pause to change my leader tippet to 4X, I turned around and began to work upstream, this time with a buoyant Coachman Trude—a fly that looks more like a hot fudge sundae than a bug but seems to interest the fish.

The upstream leg was not a chuck-and-chance- it affair. Since I had already marked several trout that showed at my wet flies but didn't take, I could concentrate on pockets that I knew held fish. This made wading against the current worth the effort. I fished a short line again, often with nothing more than half the leader on the good water. It was also easier to hold a hooked fish in the pocket, although one good brown trout did dash downstream between my legs, which caused a momentary loss of dignity.

Reaching the upstream end of the pocket water, I sat down on a comfortable-looking rock and began to eat my long-forgotten lunch. A shoal of sparkling sand had built up in the eddy behind the rock, and a small patch of foam twirled, forming and reforming, against it. Looking more closely, I could make out the pebble cases of caddis clinging to the rock, and just above the waterline, the dry husks of several large stoneflies. Although I couldn't see them, I knew blackfly larvae also lived in the rapids, clinging to the rocks with tiny hooks stronger than steel. That was why blackflies were so numerous along trout stream rapids during the first warm days of spring.

Despite the bright sunlight, it was dark and cool between the rocks, and except for the bright little shoal, it was hard to see into the water through the ever-changing surface currents. I could see small whorls as bits of sand were swept up and redeposited, and there were several tiny insects trapped in the patch of foam. The pocket water was a real trout cafeteria—plus whatever unlucky bugs had lost their grip somewhere upstream and were tumbling helplessly in the passing current.

I have faith in the Coachman and the Dark Cahill for this kind of fishing, but anything small and suggestive of life would be effective in such a spot, where the trout had only a moment to decide whether to stay home or dash out and eat. For the more cautious or reluctant fish, the sight of two juicy bugs swimming and darting within range, just under the surface, was at least worth a closer look, especially after the big hatches were over for the season. And as for the Coachman Trude—well, what fish could resist a hot fudge sundae on a summer day? Five more willing customers had confirmed that, and all were pretty good ones for this stream, between ten and 14 inches, thick and well fed.

As I gathered myself up to hike out to the railroad grade, I thought this sort of fishing would seem very old-fashioned to my hatch-matcher friends back downstream in the big pool. But they could fish to their heart's content—and maybe even catch a fish or two when the sun finally left the water. Then they could tell their buddies back home how the trout would only take a #22 emerger.

For myself, I was happy in the pocket water.

The Right Fly

Most fly fishers proceed happily through life with a vision constantly before them—that magic time when there's a good hatch, trout are rising, and they have the Right Fly to match the hatch. Such situations make up the bulk of the articles in the fly fishing magazines. Unfortunately, they seem to be rare in real life—at least in my real life.

Nevertheless, this vision drives many anglers to buy even more flies and more and more exotic fly-tying materials, searching for flies which are supposed to imitate these hatches. They read entomology books, learn to pronounce *Stenonema fuscum* and *Tricorythodes*, and attend fly fishing seminars presented by revered experts in the field. I have done all of this myself for almost 50 years—so sustaining is that vision of the right hatch and the Right Fly. Of course, over the years I have accumulated many such flies, most of which have sat idle in my fly boxes, awaiting their big moment—which never seems to come along.

Last spring I thought I had come close to realizing this vision. I was told about sure-fire hatch of little sulphur mayflies and tied up some special dry flies—size #16, pale yellow beaver fur body, upright deer hair wing, and a few with parachute hackles for heavier water. Overzealous as usual, I tied up two dozen of these and had them in a separate fly box, along with several pheasant tail emerger nymphs, all arranged in neat ranks.

I was fishing through some riffle water after wading around some large boulder, picking off the occasional trout with a Coachman Trude, a fly that looks like nothing in nature but has usually worked for me. Then I saw some little yellow mayflies starting to ride the current, bobbing along like a miniature regatta before taking wing and fluttering to the streamside bushes. Soon the trout began to rise.

"At last!" I thought. "This is the sulphur hatch, and I have the Right Fly." I clipped off the Coachman Trude, tied on a new tippet, fumbled for my new fly box, and picked out one of my freshly tied little sulphur duns. I tied it on carefully, dressed the wing with flotant, and looked around for a fish to cast to.

Trout were coming to the little flies regularly now, and I covered a nearby rise. A planter from last fall confidently took on the first drift, and I released a nine-inch brown trout a few moments later. Now that I clearly had the Right Fly, I shouldn't waste it on tiddlers. I needed to find the Right Fish.

Conflicting maxims ran through my head: "big rise, small fish," or "big rise, big fish," or "small rise, big fish," or small rise, small fish." Now that it seemed all the trout in the river were rising, how could I pick out a big one? Doubts loomed large as I glanced around from one rise to another.

Finally I settled on a steady riser holding just at the edge of a current seam, a few feet downstream from a big boulder. I waded into position, made a quartering cast upstream, and tensed for the rise. The Right Fly floated down unmolested. A few seconds later, the trout rose again.

The currents were complex, and it was hard to get a drag-free drift, but I cast again. Changed position slightly, cast again, and yet again. Each time the Right Fly was ignored. Soon losing faith, I changed to another one, same pattern, but a bit lighter in color, perhaps slightly closer to the little sailboats drifting past me.

Another cast with the Right Fly, and again nothing. I cast across to another riser and promptly hooked a second 9-inch planter—a trout I probably could have caught with a bluegill popper. Meanwhile, the fish I really wanted rose again. I cast again, mending for a better drift, and again the fly floated down without incident.

Maybe an emerger is the real Right Fly, I thought. So I clipped off the dun, fumbled around through my fly boxes again, and tied on an emerger nymph. It was a lot harder to see, but I hadn't reeled up, so I was confident I could cast accurately to the same spot and get a good drift. Several fruitless casts later, my confidence was ebbing fast. Meanwhile, the trout continued to rise all around me, and it was getting dark.

I put up the little sulphur dry fly again, shifted position to change the casting angle, and tried again—and again, nothing. I thought of moving to another spot, but the light wasn't going to last much longer. Finally, in desperation, I clipped off the cursed sulphur dun and tied on the Coachman Trude, mashed and neglected on the lamb's-wool patch pinned to my vest. I had to hold it up to the sky to poke the tippet through the hook eye. Then I blew hard on it to fluff it up a bit, turned to the still-rising trout, and made a cast.

You can guess what happened. The trout came up, ate the Coachman Trude on the first drift, and dashed out of the pocket and across the main current. The reel began to screech, and then everything fell slack. I reeled up to find the fly gone, and in its place a coiled pigtail where the knot, tied in haste and in the dark, had pulled through.

But at least I had finally found the Right Fly.

Spinner Fall

I arrived on the river just as the sun was leaving the water. Although it was early June, the weather was already warm, and the trout were unlikely to be doing much through the bright midday hours.

Wading this stretch was ticklish. The spring runoff scours deep holes around the glacial boulders, and it is all too easy to step from a shallow gravel bar into a three-foot hole. Even with good light, I had some unsteady moments as I waded upstream toward a promising riffle below a staircase of frothy rapids.

There wasn't much happening, so I put up a Hairwing Coachman, just to have something to do. But I was hoping for a Gray Drake spinner fall, which would surely draw some good fish to the surface. Old hands spoke reverently of the Gray Drake, but big brown trout were picky, rarely coming to a dry fly, and wading a big river in darkness could be dangerous.

The Gray Drake is an oddity among mayflies, because the duns do not emerge on the stream surface like other mayflies. Instead, they crawl out on the bank, more like a stonefly, and spread their wings on dry land. But their mating flight is over the water, where the spinners dance and ultimately fall spread-eagled to the surface—and the trout are waiting for them.

When do they fall? No one could say for sure. For those anglers with a lifetime on the river there may be natural clues, but for occasional visitors like myself, it was mostly a matter of luck. But I kept looking up, hoping to see the spinners whirling and dancing above my head. The early evening had light winds and an encouraging touch of humidity. However, I had seen only two other anglers, well downstream of the big boulders—not a good sign on a well-known river with plenty of local experts.

A rise to the Hairwing Coachman jolted me out of these speculations, and I was lucky to hook up. But a slow strike is often better than a quick one, and I soon had a handsome 12-inch brown trout in the net.

As I stooped to release the fish, I glanced toward the sky again—and there they were, the Gray Drake spinners, fluttering soundlessly out of the trees, dropping down and rising again like little kites.

Suddenly I was all thumbs as I clipped off the Coachman and tied on a fly I hoped would suggest a spinner. But my hurrying was for naught—the Gray Drakes still danced several feet above my head, and nothing broke the surface.

There! Not twenty feet away, a head-and-tail rise, and then another. The spinners were beginning to fall, and the trout were moving to them.. I cast a few feet above the rise. I could barely see the fly, but I could gauge its drift. The head-and-tail rise came again.

It was another 12-inch fish, and I shamelessly horsed it in, netted it quickly and popped out the fly with none of the usual admiring looks, hurrying to blow the water off the splayed wings and cast again. With every minute I was losing light, but I could still see the spinners dancing nearer, just above my head.

Moving a few feet upstream, I saw a little spritz of water in the riffle. As first I didn't recognize it, but then I realized that a trout's tail had flung it up. It came again in a few moments, and then again. I moved to get a better angle and cast. The fly promptly sank, but as I cursed my luck, the spritz came again, and without thinking I tightened up to the slow thump-thump of a heavy fish. The light rod bucked with every head-shake. I managed to reel up the slack before the trout decided to move, and when it did, it swam slowly and doggedly across the riffle, pulling against the click of the reel.

I thought the trout would bolt downriver for the safety of the boulders, but it held steady, then moved upstream. I stepped further into the riffle, trying to get a downstream angle so it would fight the current. It stopped 25 feet away, and again I felt a thumping as it tried to rub out the fly on the bottom.

For a few minutes it was a standoff. The trout held its position, the little rod arced and throbbed, and I neither gained nor lost line. I thought of adding pressure to turn the fish, but if I did it would surely blow past me and break off in the rocks downstream. Instead of moving the fish to me, I decided, I'll move to it. I unclipped my net and began to wade up behind it, reeling a few turns with each step.

The water was little more than knee deep, and when the trout rolled heavily on the surface, the leader was in the rod guides. I froze up, not knowing what to do. Finally, greatly daring, I lifted the rod. The trout surged downstream, and instinctively I stabbed the net into the water.

The trout hit the net like a hot ground ball, and when I lifted it clear, its tail and a third of its body were still outside the frame. I stumbled to the current edge, put the net back in the water and felt for the fly. The trout lay unmoving, then boiled away as I reversed the net and set him free. It was a big male with jaws like a nutcracker.

As the trout disappeared back into the riffle, I was suddenly weak and sat down with an awkward crunch on the gravel, the chewed-up Gray Drake spinner still clamped in my forceps. A moment later I was startled by a voice. "You O.K.?" a shadowy figure asked. One of the anglers I saw down below the big boulders had come up toward me.

"Yeah," I said, still breathing hard, "just a little shaky."

"Those big ones'll do that to ya," he replied. "Why don't you follow me back? It's getting pretty dark."

I looked up at the twilight. The sky was clear, and the dancing spinners were gone. "Thanks." I said. "I believe I will."

Spring Creeks

The robins in the valley began to sing at first light, though fog still hung over the river, and a heavy dew had gathered on the grass and condensed on the windows of my truck cap. I had driven far across the state to the driftless area to renew acquaintances with its spring creeks and decided to set up for the night at the campground in Avalanche—the name a reminder of the old days, of flash flood waters careening down the steep, logged-off valleys, sweeping all before them.

After a quick breakfast I rolled up my sleeping bag and drove to a meadow stream which meandered in and out of pastureland and hardwoods. DNR workers, landowners and local volunteers had done much to repair banks once torn away by flood waters or broken down by cattle, and the stream ran clear and cold over bright sand and thick brownish-green weeds.

The valley, indeed, the whole driftless region, reminded me of the south of England—lush meadows, carefully tended gardens, wooded hilltops, and fertile limestone streams. There were red barns and white farmhouses enough for a hundred calendar photographs—some newly painted and op- timistic, others more careworn and discouraged-looking.

Up close, there were differences—rosemaling on farm signs and mailboxes, the lilt of a Norwegian accent among the old-timers in the coffee shop, the sharp gabled roofs, the antique farm engines, and cows instead of sheep on the grassy slopes. But the creeks themselves were very much like the Itchen and the other British chalk streams, and their resident brown trout could be every bit as difficult.

In freestone steams, the hurly-burly of the current can hide the angler from the trout, but in this smooth water, with little bankside cover, I had to crawl through the meadow grass around cowflops old and new to work into a casting position at the first bend. The fog had dissipated, the light was good, and I could see several trout holding in the current over the weeds, feinting left and right as bits of food drifted to them. Behind me, dozens of violets nodded to the morning breeze.

There was no surface activity yet, so I put on a slim little peacock nymph, greased the long leader down to the tippet, and cast as gently as possible above a good fish. As so often happens, the trout ignored my nymph, but I let it wash down along the limestone rocks, saw the leader hesitate, and promptly hooked up on an unseen fish. The throbbing rod told me it was a big one, and I scrambled to my feet, clumsy with excitement.

The trout had allies down among the rocks, but I managed to pull it downstream away from trouble and brought it to hand several anxious minutes later. Its dark spots looked almost as big as my little fingernail, its flanks egg-yolk yellow, its body far too thick to hold in one hand.

I admired the trout a moment, then watched as it swam slowly upstream to its hidey-hole. As I sat back among the violets and the new grass, I realized that the great British angler and dry-fly purist F.M. Halford would have harrumphed indignantly at everything I had done. I used a nymph, not a dry fly; I had not cast to a rise; and I had caught the wrong fish. Worse, I had committed the very same sins on the hallowed River Test itself. The riverkeeper there approved of nymphs but not of releasing trout, so I managed to "lose" several handsome browns. To compound the felony, I did the same thing on the Itchen, even stooping so low as to fish for grayling.

It's a commonplace for Americans to assume that British trout streams are only accessible to the moneyed elite, garbed in proper English tweeds and snooty accents. So it was with some surprise I met another decidedly un-tweedy angler on my beat who owned a small car repair garage in a near-by village. After showing me a splendid two-pound trout in his bag, he explained that he had leased a "alf rod alternate Tuesdays" on the Itchen for the past five seasons. This meant that he shared the half-mile beat every other Tuesday, and if the beat had not been taken by a tourist angler through the Rod Box tackle shop in nearby Winchester (as I had done), he could have the water himself.

His speech was far indeed from the posh accents of the elite British public schools. He seemed in every respect a local countryman, but he was no less keen on fishing than the richest aristocrat, and firmly held to the best and most correct of British angling traditions. Watching him crouch low, awaiting a rise, then casting his fly perfectly when a momentarily incautious brown trout came up, I could easily imagine I was watching G.E.M. Skues, or A.H.E. Wood, the young Roderick Haig-Brown, or even the great Halford himself.

For all the weight of British fly-fishing tradition, what I learned in those green English valleys had served me well on the spring creeks of Wisconsin—staying low, keeping out of sight, studying the drift, and making the first cast count. I suppose I had looked prayerful to other anglers passing by, but standing upright and wading was a sure way to spook the trout, so I spent most of a busy morning on my knees.

A sparse hatch of dark Hendricksons began to come on in the late morning, and the trout's attention was drawn to the surface. Still, the peacock nymph was accepted if the cast and drift were right, so I didn't change, but I did grease the leader within a foot of the fly to hold it higher in the pellucid water. Three more brown trout came to hand in the next hour.

I didn't go to an "Olde English Inne" for lunch, and unlike Izaak Walton and his long-suffering pupil Venator, I didn't hear a milkmaid's song. The only person I saw who resembled a milkmaid was driving a lawn tractor and had ears only for the music on her radio. But a lunch of brown bread and butter, locally aged cheddar cheese, and a bottle of Leinekugel beer seemed close enough to the English tradition. The purple martins and barn swallows swooped and darted over the stream, just as they had in England, making me forever glad I wasn't born a mayfly.

In the afternoon I drove to another meadow stream that was almost invisible from the roadside. This wasn't one of the more famous spring creeks. In many places it was about as wide as a doorway, and in a brisk afternoon wind it could be hard to hit the water. But it was deep and undercut, and I knew that local anglers had taken some very large browns out of it.

No room for fancy business here. I put on a fast-sinking beadhead peacock nymph and began to move quietly downstream, dropping the nymph almost at my feet on a slack line and letting the current carry it along the bottom. It was tricky to figure out how much line and leader to extend to draw the fly up just as it reached a trouty-looking hole or undercut.

Halford would not have approved of beadhead nymphs or a downstream drift, but three brown trout did—no big ones, but all better than 12 inches, and all in prime condition. To a passerby on the road it might have seemed I had taken the trout out of dry ground, so narrow was the stream. Given a few more weeks, the stream would be almost invisible under an arching roof of long grass.

Back at the general store near the campground, I admired several faded photographs of huge brown trout tucked under the glass counter-top—fish you would measure in pounds, not inches. A local landowner, hand-rolling a cigarette as he rocked in a homemade bentwood chair, said laconically, "Yep, we catch most o'them big ones on chub tails."

The great Halford would have fainted dead away. I managed to remain upright.

Trickle Trout

Late last summer I decided to scale back the complexity of my fishing for a while and go back to a little brook trout stream I had fished as a boy. The creek probably had a name on a survey map, but we called it the "Native Stream" because it held small, wild speckled trout whose red spots glowed like jewels.

I didn't go out and dig any worms like I used to, but I brought along a shirt-pocket fly box, a few splitshot, and a light eight-foot fly rod. I left my landing net and my vest of many pockets at home and carried a sandwich, an apple, and a bottle of bug dope in my fish bag.

After driving several dusty back roads, relieved that none had yet been paved, I stopped at the culvert, scrambled down the embankment, and felt the water as it murmured under the alders on its way to Lake Superior. It was cool—a good sign in August. I got back in the car and drove another

300 yards down the road, stopping near a ruined fence line, and parked on the shoulder. I never parked right at the culvert, because that would advertise the stream to passersby.

There was still a faint trace of a path along the fence line, and I walked quickly for the first 50 yards, hoping no one would see me with my rod. The aspen and birch trees stood a little apart from the trail and the fence, as if allowing them to pass. A few golden leaves were already strewn in the trail.

It was a long hike through the woods, and once I wandered off the trail and had to scout around to find it again. I realized that little remained familiar after a long absence; the trees had grown larger, balsam firs were growing up through the aspen, and there were blowdowns where none had been before. Finally the trail descended into an alder thicket. Through an opening I could see the tiny stream, dark and heavily overgrown. A miniature rapids bubbled through bracken already starting to turn brown.

After dipping up a cool drink, I began to work my way upstream. I couldn't fish more than a rod's length of line, and often I could only dap the fly into hat-size holes and pockets. After several exasperating tangles, I finally added an extra-long tippet and a splitshot, and the fly line stayed on the reel the rest of the day.

Whoever said brook trout were stupid knew nothing of these wild fish. A heavy step or an awkward movement sent wakes arrowing to cover in each little pool. With the splitshot, I could "cast" by swinging the fly back and forth and releasing a little line to shoot it forward a few feet. Most of the time I could only sneak up, poke the rod through the enfolding leaves and twigs, drop the fly into a dark hole, and twitch it back out again.

I poked and prodded my way upstream, trying to be stealthy but often stumbling or hanging up at just the wrong moment. I began to long for the open spaces and the sight of a forward cast zipping out in a graceful narrow U.

Coming to a bucket-size hole below a wad of roots, I eased up close and dropped in a fat Brown Hackle Peacock. Immediately the rod tip was yanked down, and I lifted a struggling brookie straight up, skittering on the surface. I tried to swing him in through the branches and actually got hold of him for a moment before he popped out of my hands as only a brook trout can do and was gone. Even though the fish was only nine inches, I wanted a little longer look at him before putting him back. I forgot myself for a moment and swore earnestly.

I checked the point on the Brown Hackle, found it was still sharp, and continued to poke my way upstream. Finally, where the stream almost disappeared into a leafy tunnel formed by two fallen trees, I dropped in the fly, had another immediate pull, and managed this time to bring a wriggling and squirming eight-incher to hand.

Dark-backed and strong, with white-edged fins, the native brookie lay in my hand, the ruby-red spots with their blue halos glowing as I had hoped they would. It was August, and this little male was in spawning dress, boldly marked with red along his flanks, his jaw pointed and coal black along its edges. I looked just a moment longer, held him in the current, and felt him pulse with life as he darted away.

I sat down, then, breathing hard, and unwrapped my sandwich, now mashed from my exertions in the thick brush. Peanut butter and blackberry jam goes well anywhere, and especially well in the bush. The crunch of my apple seemed almost too loud. I bent down and took another drink from the creek, feeling the cool water run through my mustache and down my neck as I straightened up.

As I sat there in silence, I saw several small warblers fluttering from branch to branch, looking under every leaf at every angle, watching for the tiniest movement. When I made a kissing noise on the back of my hand, they came closer, looking for a downed fledgling, then went back to their search for insects in the alders. A few minutes later, I saw a white-throated sparrow scratching and pecking in the duff like a farmyard hen.

I rolled to my feet again, stiff from sitting too long. It was impossible to stand upright in the tangle of branches, so I hunched over and began to work back downstream. From between two mossy boulders I caught another eight-inch native with dark purple-brown sides suffused with red, the wormlike markings on its back barely visible—coloring no artist has fully captured.

By the time I came to the trail again it was growing dark, so I didn't dare linger. A flock of crows announced my sweaty emergence from the wood, and I quickly stowed my tackle in the car, climbed in, and drove back down the road.

I paused briefly at the culvert. It was reassuring to see that the little stream was almost invisible unless you knew where to look. I have fished in many famous places since my boyhood, but I have known no greater joy than these anonymous trickles and their native trout.

Maybe next time I'll bring some worms.

The Nipigon

Though our numbers may be dwindling, there are still some of us for whom the brook trout is the quintessential trout—a brightly colored embodiment of grace and glowing color no artist has every quite captured. The little brookies of the north woods were perhaps too easy to catch, and they have been supplanted by brown trout and rainbows in many watersheds, but a few can still be found.

Brookies are generally small, six to ten inches or so. Their presence in tiny streams is a sign of a clean, relatively undisturbed environment, but often brushy and difficult to fish. When we see them darting about, we are re-minded of a boyhood in creeks speckled with sunlight, where in bucket-size pools brook trout rose confidently to flies vaguely suggesting mayflies and caddis larvae or perhaps just something alive. The problem of getting the fly on the water was often more difficult than the choice of a fly (or worm). But let a booted foot land too heavily on streamside boulder, or push a shady limb too far to the side, and they could vanish like smoke.

For some of us who long ago graduated to fly fishing in bigger rivers, these boyhood adventures with simple tackle may well have been the happiest fishing we have known. Now, as we watch the water, hoping to see a swirl, our thoughts drift northward to a more primitive land, a land of moose and muskegs, storm-battered trees, and bright orange lichens splashed on rocks over a billion years old.

There are a few such places—rough, primitive places, where brook trout grow to ferocious size, with the gaping maw large enough to swallow a mouse, or even a lemming. Here brook trout compete with lake trout and northern pike for the limited bounty of the Far North. In these rivers brook trout live, not in quiet, sunlit pools and sparkling riffles, but in rivers swift and dangerous, with boiling current and upwellings that threaten to overturn small boats. Here we might see days and days of steely skies, strong winds and heavy waves sweeping across large and forbidding lakes.

No idle talk of dainty rises and sun-dappled pools here. This is rugged country, a land of hard rocks and steep cliffs, where the huge blocks of stone tumble down steep slopes to disappear in clear, deep water, where dark coniferous trees claw a meager existence from cracks and crevices in the bare rock.

The Cree people called it *Nipigon* (deep clear water lake). A few of the boys who grew up fishing for speckled trout in tiny creeks become men, tough and rugged themselves, who risk everything in a harsh land of violent rapids and deep, cold lakes. Even the names of their streams reflect the difference. Simple local names like Elm Creek, Bally Creek and Rocky Run fit the simple rural Minnesota landscape well, and some have no names at all. But such intimacy is not to be found in names that sweep across vast, largely unexplored northern watersheds, names like Minipi, Gods River, Kaniapiscau, or the storied Nipigon.

The Nipigon! Can there be a more evocative name for any place on earth? How appropriate it is that in 1916 the world record brook trout, a giant of 14 ½ pounds, was caught in the Nipigon, for it is a land of giants, of Nature writ large, bold, and primitive. To hold a brook trout from this place is to reach back in time, to see the continent laid bare, as it was after the last glaciers, to sense the raw power of the ice as it is reshaped rocks already more than a billion years old.

With eagerness but also some trepidation a friend and I persuaded a few friends and relatives to undertake a trip to the Nipigon. We chartered the *Nipigon Discovery*, a 60-foot vessel accommodating six to eight passengers, a captain who doubled as guide, and towing three sturdy open boats powered by 15-horsepower outboard motors. Our complement was six passengers, with different skills and experience, but with equal fascination for the rugged terrain and the challenges it would present. Nipigon is the largest lake in Ontario, and it is often called the "Sixth Great Lake," for it is 62 miles wide, 44 miles long, covering over 2,700 square miles, and 450 feet deep at its deepest.

Into this forbidding land we brought the tools of modern angling--the rods, reels, lines, flies, and lures of another place and time--only to find many of them inadequate to the task. A five-weight fly rod simply cannot handle a big brook trout in heavy current. A light spinning rod with six pound test line is no match for the speckled trout that might be attracted to the flash of gold spinner blades.

We lived aboard the boat, and with good reason. The shoreline was so rough it defied camping in all but a few places. Each night we found a quiet anchorage; each day we ventured out to fish promising shorelines, focusing on the depths where the rocky bottom could just barely be seen. We didn't know where the brook trout might hold in preparation for spawning. Trolling these shorelines, we covered a lot of water, but found no pattern that would tell us how we might concentrate our effort. The first afternoon we caught a few big brook trout (four to six pounds or better) in heavy current near a broken-down dam. Despite how near the rapids were, there was a quiet area nearby and there we anchored for the night.

In the morning of the second day, after we gave the rapids another try, the captain decided we should make a long run to the northern islands, so we ran several hours into the wind to get there. The plan was to reach water that would not be pounded into froth by onshore winds. And so we began a long trek with only occasional shelter from the islands that we passed. The captain spoke of a spawning sanctuary for brook trout. We couldn't fish there, but we could nearby. Our anticipation was keen- this area was remote and lightly fished, and there were big northern pike as well as big brook trout, whitefish, and small walleyed pike. The captain said the fishing was even better than at the tumble-down dam we had fished earlier.

But by late afternoon it was becoming clear that our captain was ill. At first he simply covered up to stay warm and tried to indicate where we might go for some more big trout. But we found it difficult to interpret his advice, and we caught only a few fish. However, he was able to get us halfway close, and our experience took over from there. At nightfall we anchored in a narrows below a rapids and caught a baker's dozen small walleye to eat. We shared the anchorage with another mothership. Several white pelicans had taken up residence in the swirls and eddies of the rapids, and a bald eagle circled watchfully overhead. During the night a violent storm and bright lightning awakened us, but we were safe inside a deep narrows below the rapids.

On the morning of the third day we caught a few brook trout from four to six pounds, two big northern pike, and a five-pound whitefish. We had to cope with rough water at every moment. Other lures or flies might have worked better in calmer water. We lost a few lures to powerful northern pike that signaled nothing but a light tick as they rolled near the surface and cut the leader.

The brook trout we brought to hand were not numerous—a total of eight or ten trout from four to six pounds—but they were large and colored as we had hoped they would be, with spawning colors that looked almost gaudy until we held them under water, where they blended perfectly with the ever shifting mix of colors and wave action. Walleyed pike were small but plentiful for camp fare. From another boat came rumors of a 40-pound lake trout caught a few days earlier, but surface temperatures were in the 60s—too warm for anything except deep trolling with downriggers. We thought we might give that a try later in the week. After all, the current record for Lake Nipigon is 55 pounds, and reportedly a 70-pounder was taken in commercial nets a few years ago.

The third day brought strong winds from a direction that made fly-fishing difficult. We had made a few desultory casts with fly tackle, but we soon switched to spinning and baitcasting gear so that we could cover more water more quickly and try to find out where the brook trout were. We concluded that the big fish were widely scattered and still far away from their spawning gravel. We were equipped for several different strategies, and it would not have been difficult to rig two or three downriggers to see what might be going on in deeper water. Meanwhile, our captain's condition grew worse and worse. In an early afternoon meeting we decided that we had no choice but to forgo any more fishing and run the heavy waves to get the captain back to town for medical treatment. One of our group had substantial experience in big water, so he was at the wheel for more than three hours. We piloted our sixty-foot vessel ourselves most of the way, but we still had to lift the captain to the wheel to navigate difficult areas. We were all very much aware that what might start as a simple infection could have become deadly in that country, especially if we became windbound. As it was, even with a sturdy 60-foot boat we would lurch as rogue waves struck it from unexpected angles, so we dared not leave the wheel, even for a few moments, without someone else there to take over.

Several hours passed before we saw the lights of Orient Bay. It was too dark to see channel marker buoys, so once again we had to lift the captain to the wheel to point the way through the channel. But we came back safely, knowing as perhaps we had not known before how precarious our lives were in this land of big water and hard rocks. In a way, we had lost our innocence. We would never again watch small brook trout finning gracefully in a tiny creek without thinking also of the dark side of the brook trout-- large, voracious, primordial—that we had seen and touched in the Nipigon.

V

Wonders

The Cannibal

There always seem to be some spots in a trout stream that look as if they ought to hold fish but never produce—never a rise, never even a sign of a fish. Such places are troubling, especially when you think you have finally begun to understand the movement of water and where the trout hold and feed.

One pool comes to mind immediately. The stream isn't large, and much of it runs through open country, with brush and alders in the low spots where the bank is soft. The current sweeps in strongly through a shallow riffle and the bottom drops away into deep water under the curving arm of the bank. A snaggly alder has fallen part-way in, and years of flowing water have torn away most of its bark. In the summer, grasses trail in the water, further shading the undercut. A patch of foam twirls endlessly in an eddy behind the half-sunk bush.

The path (nowadays there's always a path) is on the deep side, but it swings wide of this hole to avoid the alders and the grassy hummocks. Usually the path goes directly from one good spot to another, so I surmise that the other anglers have had the same dismal experience here that I have, which is to say, nothing—no rises, no fish hooked, no fish seen.

Because I couldn't stand the contradiction, I always fished through this lit-tle hole, but nothing ever showed. I remembered one of George Gordon's articles in *Outdoor Life* about the Catskill streams, where he said a place with good cover, good current, and a food supply would often be occupied by a really big trout, big enough to chase away all its competition. Gordon was a wise fisherman, but perhaps he hadn't seen a hole like this one—or maybe there were better places available for a big fish, or possibly some unpleasantness lay somewhere under the bank.

Then one day I came through again, walking the path, decided to take a look, and noticed immediately the something was different. The hole was full of small brook trout, most of them holding high in the slack water on the opposite bank, out of the main current. Upstream, toward the next pool, I saw where the grass had been newly trampled down and realized that they were freshly planted. They were too small to fish for, but I decided to sit down next to the fallen-in alder bush and watch for a while. The light was good, and I could see well into the deeper water at my feet.

I sat for several minutes, watching the little trout sampling every stick or bit of leaf the current brought their way. They hadn't yet learned to distinguish food from all the drifting stuff in the stream—it's no surprise the survival rate of stocked trout is so poor in swift streams. Still, they were fun to watch, balancing on their white-edged fins and darting here and there.

I was about to get up when I saw a brief bronze flash down deep. I wasn't sure what it was, or even that I had seen anything at all. I stayed by the bush, watching the little trout, hoping to see something more definite. Nothing showed, and I finally had to leave, but at least I had seen something to suggest I wasn't wrong about this pool. The next afternoon I hiked in across the field and went directly to the same spot. The little brook trout were still there, although there weren't as many of them. They had spread out a bit, taking up feeding stations here and there. I quietly settled down next to the scraggly bush. I sat there more than an hour, moving as little as possible, hoping to confirm what I had glimpsed the day before.

As the late afternoon sun began to drop, I couldn't see as well into the hole, but I could still make out the white-edged fins of the little brookies. Then, with a suddenness that startled me, a bold wake surged out from under the bank and turned sharply, and I saw a white mouth open and close on one of the brookies as the others scattered. It was over in an instant. As the pool quieted, the little trout gradually took up their stations again, sampling the bits of drift in the current as they had before.

I stayed until dark this time, but nothing stirred. A small flight of egg-laying caddis began as it usually did this time of year, dropping and rising, and I could hear the brook trout trying for them with splashy little rises. I had forgotten about fishing (well, almost!), and I waited to see if that frightening surge would come again. It didn't, and I finally stumbled through the hummocks back to the car.

A few days later I came back. The little brook trout were gone, and the pool was once again as empty and mysterious as it had been before. I was vaguely troubled by what I had seen. I had heard big trout chasing chubs in the shallows at night and even caught a few good ones with a big bucktail. But chubs, minnows, and sculpins were there to be eaten by trout, sort of a snack between mayflies. Trout were supposed to be graceful, dainty feeders, not lunging predators—and certainly not cannibals, devouring their own kind.

I always seem to learn something from a day on a stream, but this time I learned an uncomfortable lesson—that however we might wish it otherwise, or however much we are enthralled by their unparalleled beauty and grace, trout are in integral part of a savage, eat-or-be-eaten world. From the minnow's (or the mayfly's) point of view, a trout is another among many ravening mouths. And now I had seen for myself that trout could and did eat other trout. I also realized that, however I might wish to refine it with graceful fly rods, fine leaders, tiny flies, catch-and-release, and much talk about the art of fly-fishing, I, too, was part of that predatory world, perhaps in some ways no less to be feared than the old cannibal brown trout under the mysterious bank.

No, I never did catch him.

Jewelweed

Meteorologists are very good at predicting the movements of large weather systems, but for fishermen weather, like politics, is local, and locally it was hot, bright, and windless. Rain and cooler temperatures were predicted, which prompted me to head for the river. It had been hot for more than a month, and trout were not to be had.

So now, I thought, looking up at a bright blue sky, where's the rain? I was parboiled from hiking to the river in my waders, and the water temperature in the first riffle was in the low 70's—very warm, very low water, very bad all around.

I began working upstream, casting a soft hackle wet fly that suggested a bit of life, but not even a chub took hold. Two hours later the sky was still bright blue and the woods were hot and still. Everything was hunkered down in the heat.

As a matter of routine, I sample the water temperature in each stretch of river, so I moved on to a small bend pool, I mechanically checked it again, and found, quite by chance, that all the water was 68 degrees—not cold, but several degrees cooler than anyplace else I'd been.

I backed out of the water to the bank, pushed past some yellowish flowers, and came back into the water from further downstream. Since I had stepped blindly into the hole, I decided to wait for things to quiet down.

Staying close to the bank, I eased into casting position. I was watching the water, but then I looked again at the yellow flowers which nodded near the water's edge. They were jewelweed—two or three feet high, with soft elm-shaped leaves and curious orchid-like flower, yellow, but with orange spots and an odd hook-like structure. They dangled like Oriental lanterns from their slim, curving stems. Then I knew why the water in this pool was cooler. The jewelweed must be growing near a spring seep. The soil beneath them was black, moist, and cool to the touch.

The jewelweed is an annual, and its seedpods burst open in the fall to scatter the next generation. The dry pods pop open violently at a touch, so the plant is also called "Touch-Me-Not." But the seeds must fall on moist, rich soil, and they won't survive a dry year. A spring seep was the perfect spot for them, and here they were.

Nothing moved to the soft-hackle fly, so I changed to a weighted caddis larva—just a bit of muskrat fur with a black ostrich herl head—and cast to the quiet water, hoping it would sink right to the bottom. It did, and I crept the fly along the gravel in a slow hand-twist retrieve.

The fly line ticked and I set the hook in a 13-inch brown trout—not a big one, but a lot better than anything else I'd seen that day. I released the fish and made another cast. This time the line ticked before the fly even got to the bottom, and I soon released another trout about the same size.

Two small trout came on successive casts, and I realized I had found a trout haven. The pool was shaded, a riffle brought in oxygen and food, and the invisible spring kept the water temperature down to tolerable levels.

I decided to start looking for other patches of jewelweed, just to see if the pattern held. Since I hadn't seen anyone else on the river, I decided to wade on downstream without casting and search the banks.

I soon discovered that jewelweed didn't always grow right next to the stream. I barely glimpsed the next patch, away from the bank and hidden by some fallen trees. Probing with the thermometer, I soon found another cool seep where the temperature was in the mid 60's. I marked the spot on my map and continued downstream.

I found three more patches of jewelweed, each in a shallow valley, but the stream temperature nearby was not always cooler. One patch was near a shallow riffle, so I couldn't find any temperature difference. But of the five patches I found, two were near a pool where the water was six or eight degrees cooler.

By early evening it still hadn't rained, and no rises disturbed the water. I decided to fish one of the jewelweed pools for a few minutes on my way back to the car. Using the same very slow retrieve, I caught and released three more brown trout, one of them about 14 inches. It was obvious now—the trout were stacked in these cooler pools.

The next weekend I returned. There had been a few brief thunderstorms but no relief from the heat, and the water in the flat sunstruck pool was still close to 75 degrees. I started to walk upstream to see if I could find other patches of jewelweed, but then my desire to catch a fish got the better of me, and I headed back to the pool where I had first noticed them.

I put on the gray caddis larva and cast to the area where I knew the water was coolest. Right on cue, the leader ticked and I hooked a good trout, better than 14 inches, and managed to clear it out of the pool downstream a few yards before the hook pulled out. Two casts later, I had another fish on, brought it quickly to net—another nice brown, about 12 inches—and held it in the water to release it.

The second trout didn't dart away quite as fast as I expected, and as I straightened up, I realized something was wrong. While the seep areas were cooler, the trout were still stressed by the warm water, and I was just adding to their problems. Besides, I thought, it's too easy now. The mystery was gone, and I had an unfair advantage.

So, although I still look for patches of jewelweed in the summer, I don't fish any more when to water gets too warm.

It's enough to know where the trout are and that they're O.K.

The Log Bridge

The spring woods were warm and full of life as I tramped along a narrow trail. I had attracted an insistent following of mosquitoes and blackflies, and once or twice I swept my hat across my shoulders in a futile gesture to ward them off. There had been little rain and fishing was poor, but I was going to try one more creek before heading home.

The trail eventually led across an old bridge. The tiny, nameless stream that ran between its crumbling logs and braces seemed unworthy of the time and effort that had gone into building it, but the undercut along the bottom logs was almost a sure bet for at least one decent brook trout. I crept close and dapped on a wet fly over the edge with just enough line to drift it a few feet.

The first trout darted out in a quick half turn, grabbed the fly, and headed back under the log. There was no place to play the fish, so I simply derricked it out, hoping the leader would hold. The trout was splendid in the sunlight, dark-backed and bronzy purple, its red spots glowing—a native fish for sure.

Usually the bridge was good for only one trout of any size, as the commotion of taking one would spook the others, but this time I soon had two ten-inchers wrapped in moist ferns and tucked away in my bag. My plan was to cross the bridge on its one remaining cross-log and continue down the trail another half mile to a larger stream, but walking on that narrow log was no small undertaking for one whose balance was notoriously uncertain.

I was gathering my courage to cross when I happened to see a faint splash of pale purple beyond a thick stand of aspen and small balsam firs. I had walked the trail and stopped at the bridge many times, but I hadn't noticed this before. I took my rod down and pushed through the heavy brush for a closer look.

As I stepped clear of the thickly grown aspen, I saw it was a large lilac bush in full bloom, and there were several others nearby. At first I couldn't believe that lilacs would be growing out here in the woods, but as I looked around, I could see the vague outline of what was once a clearing.

Walking closer, I stumbled over the stone remains of a cellar wall. Just beyond it, near the lilacs, I could see several squared and rotting logs and the remains of a collapsed roof. I was standing in the middle of an old farmstead which had been taken over long ago by the surrounding second growth.

Starting at the largest lilac bush, I began to walk in a slow spiral around and around, scuffing through the grass and brush. I soon found a broken wagon wheel, its rim thick with rust. A little further on, I found the remains of a small outbuilding. It too had completely collapsed and was almost invisible, but I recognized the style of the notched corners and knew it was built by a Finnish settler. I walked on in an ever widening circle, but there was nothing more.

Returning to the lilacs and the cellar hole, I tried to visualize the farm as it had once stood—a sauna, a simple log home built tightly of hand-hewn logs to withstand the winter winds, a barn or shed of some kind, a horse to pull the wagon, a cow or two, possibly some chickens and a dog, and a tough, wiry Finnish homesteader, his stolid square-jawed wife and three or four towheaded children.

Doubtless the homesteader and his family began their life in the clearing with the highest hopes and toiled endless hours, but somewhere along the way their hopes turned to ashes and the farm was left to fall under the steady march of the forest. Had I not caught sight of the lilacs through the trees, I might never have known the homestead ever existed. Now I could at least guess the origin of the ruined bridge, and I realized that the narrow trail was once a road.

I recalled an abandoned stretch of oiled gravel road near my boyhood home. It seemed so permanent when I rode my bicycle over it, but within just a few years after the new highway was built it was heaved, cracked, and heavily overgrown with weeds and popple saplings, speedily on its way to oblivion.

There was another ruin in the backwoods of Ontario, west of Lake Nipigon, which we found while looking for a trout stream. A large logging camp, it once teemed with hard-working, determined men. Now the roofs of the cook shack and the bunkhouse had fallen in and several walls already collapsed. The most striking remainder was a thirty-hole outhouse (yes, I counted). Among the gray and roofless buildings, we found square-forged nails, rusted saws, a grindstone, and many other tools, but we left everything just as we found it. A logging camp is temporary by definition, but the men who built those buildings could not have imagined how quickly their handiwork would sink back into the forest.

Returning through the thicket to the old bridge, I realized that the crumbling works of man were not the only marks of change. The stream itself once flowed with enough depth and power to require a substantial bridge, more than twelve feet across and head-high from the bottom gravel to the topmost log. Now it was just a trickle, barely enough to support a few trout. Perhaps, as its precious water ran off more and more quickly in the spring and nearly disappeared in the midsummer heat, the stream too would soon be nothing but a memory, its glacial boulders become headstone for its vanished trout.

Arms outspread, I teetered over the cross-log and walked further down the trail, followed once again by eager mosquitoes. As I stopped and looked back, I could almost hear the laughter of children.

The Redd

It was late October and the leaves were mostly down, forming a damp carpet of gold, brown, and red. Earlier in the season, if you kicked up a grouse you would hear the sudden thunder of wings and perhaps get a glimpse of a brown and gray, but now there was an honest chance of a shot through the branches.

It was time for the wool hunting coats, rubber-bottomed packs, and the smells of powder smoke, wet dog hair and Hoppe's No. 9. As I walked along a stream I had often fished during the summer, my eyes were not on the water as they were then, but on the low growth, the blackberry tangles, and the black Labrador ahead of me.

As I watched the dog lap and drink from a shallow riffle, I saw a swirl in the pool ahead, just downstream of a big jackpine that leaned far over, supported above the current by its broken branches. Noon was approaching, so I decided its thick trunk would be a good place to sit, eat lunch, and watch the water.

I whistled in the dog, broke and unloaded the light 20-gauge shotgun, and pulled out my lunch from my game pocket. The dog had worked hard all morning and flopped down gratefully on the leaves. It can be tough to keep up with a Lab in grouse country, and I was breathing harder than he was.

The swirl came again as I opened the paper bag and brushed away a couple of matted grouse feathers. It didn't look like a rise, and there were no bugs this late in the year, so I was prompted to watch more closely.

The morning had been mostly overcast, but now a patch of blue sky showed through the clouds, and sunlight illuminated the pool for a few moments—enough for me to see several brook trout holding together over the gravel bottom. Golden aspen leaves twirled in the current or clung to the bottom near the tailout. Then the sky darkened again.

Since the pine was tipped well down, I could move out over the water for a better view. I put away my sandwich, told the dog to stay, and crept out on the trunk. There were a couple of branches to steady me, and I worked my out until I was close to where I had seen the fish.

Looking almost straight down, I could see all five of them clearly as the sun came out again. Two of them swung out and away, dropping downstream, but then they came back and held close together. Then I saw why they were reluctant to leave: a female brookie turned on her side and dug furiously at the bottom for a few seconds. A puff of sand, silt and gravel rose and shifted downstream with the current.

As the sunlight revealed the lighter color of freshly turned gravel, I realized she had been digging her redd for some time. Another trout rolled close by, a male, splendid in his spawning colors. He turned from his break and chased one of the small fish, then returned to his position just behind and to the left of the female, who turned on her side again and wriggled vigorously forward, stirring up another cloud of sand and gravel.

I watched for several minutes as the patch of lighter-colored gravel grew larger. Now and then one of the smaller fish would try to come close to her, only to be driven off by the biggest male. The dog whined behind me, and I turned to see him sitting up and watching me. "Stay," I said again.

The female trout stopped digging and held steady now, very near the bottom, the male close beside her. Another bright patch of sunlight illuminated them both, and I realized they were about to spawn. They started to press very close together, and then another cloud obscured the sun, as if to give them some privacy.

When the light returned again a few moments later, the female was digging again further upstream. Her exertions must have already covered her eggs, for I could see no pale orange orbs on the bottom. I watched for a while longer, then moved slowly back to the bank.

Back home that night, sitting before the fireplace with the dog sound asleep at my feet, I thought again of the trout and the spawning. It was a sign of a healthy stream, and there were no fishermen to intrude. An angler who killed a trout in June had surely prevented its spawning as if he took it in September, but I was reconciled to that contradiction and was glad the trout season was closed.

It began to rain, and I was glad of that too. The summer had been dry, and though there was some scattered rain in early autumn, the streams were still low. I thought then of another spawning—not delicate or secretive like this one, but obvious and violent. The stream was not much larger, but the chinook salmon that ran in from Lake Michigan were huge, and their spawning exertions tore at the bottom and sent waves crashing into the bank.

I remembered the truck campers parked along the road, the black salmon streaked with white fungus, the trampled banks, the snarls of fluorescent blue line in the bushes, the shouts and curses. "They die anyway," I was told a hundred times by men with strong rods and weighted treble hooks.

That argument prevailed for several years, but as the damage and disruption spread, the snagging finally became intolerable, at least in the eyes of the law.

Still, I wondered, why would someone who yanked a treble hook through spawning salmon in years past think differently of the brook trout in their spawning? "They die anyway" is true for them too, for brookies do not live very long, and those I watched below me would probably not make it through the winter if the water stayed low. Would he be tempted to return with treble hooks to the big pine?

Or would he sit quietly watching the redd and wonder at the miracle of gravel, sunlight, and flowing water?

Snakes

The quiet of the morning had given way to a busier time, and the roar of outboard motors combined with the sloshing of boat wakes against the beach. The reeds and lily pads swayed crazily in the rush of water, and I could no longer stand up to cast.

I paddled further offshore, drifted over some cabbage weed, and cast again with a weedless spoon and pork strip. Normally I fished it near the surface, even skipping it from pad to pad, but now I let it drop into the deeper weeds, fluttering the trailing porkrind.

A sudden yank brought everything to a stop, and I was fast in a strong fish. With the wind coming up, I had an anchor tied off and ready, and I lifted and dropped it overboard as the canoe began to broach. The next several minutes were busy, but I kept the fish clear of the weeds and finally lifted it aboard—a northern pike of eight or nine pounds, its fins bright orange, its jaws clamped tight on the spoon.

Another boat drifted close behind me as I fought the pike of the weeds, and as I lifted it over the gunwale, it came closer still. "Whadja get?" shouted the two anglers as I reached for the pliers and began to pry out the lure.

"A northern," I said, turning and holding it up to the sunlight.

"Oh, jeez, a damned snake," said one of them. "The DNR oughta clean them things outa here once and for all!" They cranked up their outboard and moved off in disgust. I was too busy extracting my spoon to reply. As I released the fish, I was reminded again that many anglers hate northern pike—a fish that seems to radiate malevolence, its jaws designed to gobble walleyes or helpless ducklings, or to slash the fingers of unwary fishermen.

For myself, I was glad to hook a good-size northern in prime condition, and also puzzled by the attitudes anglers have toward fish in various parts of the country. In Minnesota, the yellow perch is a trash fish, while in Wisconsin, its tender fillets are highly prized as part of a long tradition of Friday night fish fries. To the walleye fisherman, a bass is a nuisance, while to the bass fisherman 50 yards away, it is the gamest fish that swims. A barracuda on the winter bonefish flats is the target of fervent curses—unless it is hooked by a Midwestern newcomer who stares open-mouthed as the cuda's blistering first run nearly empties his reel.

I was reminded of another northern pike I caught as a boy. My father was not one to make long-range fishing plans, so we found ourselves driving around the lake country visiting resorts in search of a vacancy. I grew impatient with all the stops, so when we pulled in at yet another lodge, I put together my old bamboo fly rod, tied on a wet fly, and began to cast from the dock, hoping for a couple of bluegills. As it happened, a four-pound pike ambushed the fly and dashed into the weeds. The crooked old Montague rod wheezed, but eventually I slid the pike up onto the grassy beach. One look at that mouthful of teeth and I called for help.

The man who ran over to me had been cleaning fish, and his hands were spangled with scales as he grabbed my northern behind the head. "These slimy hammer-handles are everywhere," he exclaimed as he tore the fly loose.

Here was the biggest fish I had caught on a fly, and my pride in its capture turned instantly to ashes. Later, sitting before the fireplace at the lodge and trying hard to fit in with the grownups, I too began to talk of northern pike as "snakes" and "hammer-handles."

I recalled another long-ago day, when college students still had to have a faculty chaperone on field trips, so even though in my first year of teaching I was only a little older than the students, I had been invited along on a weekend canoe trip. As we paddled down the lake, we decided to fish a little on the way to the campsite. Approaching a wooded island, I chanced to see a big pike holding just off a gravel point—lurking, I should say. I had a spinning outfit set up, and I said to the student in the bow, "Want to see that fish hit this plug?"

He had never seen such a big fish, and he was all eyes as I cast beyond the point and retrieved the lure a few feet away from the pike's snout. There was a good chance of getting cut off, but it would be fun to see the strike.

Right on cue, the pike darted forward, seized the Rapala, and bolted for deep water. Luckily, she did not completely engulf the lure, so my six-pound test monofilament escaped injury. After several long minutes I had the fish next to the canoe.

My popeyed companion turned into the bow seat, forgetting all deference to his scholarly chaperone. "Man, you gonna grab that thing? Look at those teeth!"

It was a difficult bit of business, and twice the pike surged away at my touch, but finally I managed to get my hand under a gill cover, grasped its jaw from the inside, and lifted it partway out so I could get out the hooks.

"She's much too big to keep," I said. "We'll just let'er go." And with that I put the fish back, cradling it as it hung motionless. Then it lunged away, splashing me with a faceful of water.

Later, in the evening firelight, the student retold with dramatic gestures how the big northern lay in wait in the shallows, how it attacked the lure and leaped ferociously near the canoe, slashing left and right with its vicious teeth. The other students were suitably impressed, the co-eds in particular, and I imagine the fish grew a lot bigger when the story got back to the dormitories on campus.

But pike are the stuff of legend, so it may have grown a bit in my mind too.

Snapping Turtle

It had been a tough day of rain, wind, and scudding clouds. My wife and I were wet and tired as we beached the canoe, tipped out the rainwater, and scrambled over the slick rocks to rig a tarpaulin and get out of the weather. Along the opposite shore, the multicolored cliffs dissolved into sheets of gray as yet another rainstorm swept across the open water.

Finally the rain relented, and we threw the tent up, ate a quick meal of cheese and summer sausage on cold biscuits, and slung the bear bag between two dripping trees. The sky remained a steely gray, but there was a faint brightening in the west. Walking the shoreline near the campsite, I saw a school of smallmouth bass in a little basin, very close to the shore. I was turning to go and get my rod when the sun came out beneath the cloud wrack, and the school moved as one into deeper water, out of sight.

The wind had lessened considerably, and we could see the weather would fair off before nightfall. We spread our rain gear out to dry and walked down to the water's edge. A narrow "elephant back" of bare basaltic rock sloped down into the water, and we sat down on our life jackets to watch the sunset. The rock was like a bare rib of the continent showing through the duff. We could see the striations that marked the long-ago passage of the last glacier.

I had just begun to remark the age of the lava flow beneath us when an enormous snapping turtle appeared, swimming with infinite slowness along the rock, just under the surface. We could see its mossy shell and outstretched neck plainly as it dipped down and nosed the bottom rubble. Then, just a few feet away, it rose to breathe, looking at us with an unblinking eye. We exhaled together as it sank from sight, a creature seemingly as ancient as the rocks themselves.

There are encounters in nature that cheer us—the bright songs and fluttering displays of courting birds in spring, the leap of a bass at a dragonfly, the thunder of a drumming grouse, the scuffle of pine squirrels harvesting cones. We exult the gladness in living that these creatures seem to express and find ourselves refreshed by the experience. Even the mud turtles sunning themselves on exposed logs evoke a laugh as they stretch their striped necks and flop head-long into the water as the canoe approaches.

But there are other, less cheering encounters—cold reminders that the natural world is neither joyous nor friendly. Yet they too have a fascination, and like a bird transfixed by the lidless eyes of a snake, we watch, unable to tear our glance away.

My wife gripped my arm as the snapping turtle's head emerged again at the surface a little further away. She was not reassured when I told her how, long ago, another snapping turtle had eaten a full stringer of walleyes we had kept tied to the dock while the livebox was being repaired. We caught that one later and brought it home, where we kept it in a laundry tub for a few days. Not wasting the opportunity, I charged a nickel admission to let the neighbor kids watch the turtle crunch the landlord's broom handles. (Business was brisk but short-lived—my profits went to replace the brooms, and so did my allowance.) We were fascinated by the power of those terrible jaws, so unlike the tiny painted turtles in the dime-store.

I get much the same uneasy feeling when I pass rookeries of shore birds like pelicans or cormorants—their long beaks, their raucous calls, their awkward flapping and clambering among the branches, their unblinking eyes and the reptilian look of their heads and necks—a feeling quite different from seeing a chickadee or a flock of geese or a pair of sandpipers running back and forth on the beach.

Most fish don't frighten me, even some of the snaggle-toothed predators like northern pike or barracuda, but sharks are another matter. Once, poling the flats of Biscayne Bay in Florida, we saw a commotion on the surface. Running over with the skiff, we came upon a 14-foot hammerhead shark chasing an eagle ray. The skiff drifted almost on top of the shark. Its dorsal fin was thrust far above the surface, within a rod's length of the gunwale, but it paid no attention to us. Desperate to escape, the ray swooped and turned with incredible speed. The shark matched its every move, gaining at every turn. Finally they both disappeared into a deeper channel, but I have no doubt of the outcome of that relentless chase.

I tried to make light of the spectacle: "Well, I'm glad that shark had "Eat ray!" on its mind and not "Eat Don!", but the joke rang hollow, and the guide and I stared in silence at the frothy water. Afterward, it was hard to concentrate on searching for bonefish. I kept thinking about the myriad life-and-death battles going on in the sand and turtle grass beneath the skiff.

Sitting on that ancient rock and watching the sun touch the horizon, it was harder to think about, but as we waited for the turtle to show itself again, we knew the same desperate struggle for life was going on beneath the placid surface of the lake—sunfish nipping water fleas, bass gobbling crayfish and the horrible jaws of the turtle ready to snatch at any of them, should they stray too near. I felt my wife shiver, and though we were no longer cold, I decided a campfire would be comforting.

I suppose one reason we fish and camp is to get close to nature—but not too close. That unblinking stare is too unsettling, and ultimately we must look away, back into the firelight.

Water Music

Fishing, and especially trout fishing, is a sport of seeing, and also somewhat of feeling or touching. How often have I heard anglers describing the look of a particular spot or seen them illustrating with arm and hand movements how they cast, retrieved, set the hook, and so on.

But to me trout fishing is also very much a sport of sounds and listening, and for that, May seems the best of all months to be wading a stream.

As I walked along a fenceline in the early morning, the new grass was probing upward through last year's dry stems. The meadowlarks sang from their fenceposts, and from a swale the redwing blackbirds responded, displaying their elegant epaulets. Several killdeer ran back and forth across a plowed field, calling each other by name.

It was still a bit early for the classic Wisconsin calendar picture of red barns, green fields, sparkling water, and black-and-white Holsteins, but life was finally astir after a cold spring, and as I followed the stream into an alder ticket, the current whispered quietly—not the boisterous plunging and bubbling of the swift freestone streams further north, but a calmer sound, like good talk in a quiet restaurant.

I was lucky even before I made a cast. Several warblers were singing in the thicket. I could hear an ovenbird's "Teacher, teacher, teacher," and I caught a glimpse of a common yellowthroat and then a redstart. Their mixture of buzzes, trills, and reedy whistles was punctuated by the clear calls of a white-throated sparrow, the "Peabody bird" that stays near the trout streams all summer.

The suggestive words of the bird books are the palest imitations of the songs of that morning. Even "Peabody," which is better than most, sounds more like the name of an accounting firm than a proclamation of vigorous life.

Since no hatch was evident, I tied on a small Hare's Ear Nymph and began to cast upstream along an undercut bank. At first I was listening more than fishing, but as I tried to work out the complex currents and get a good drift, the singing became part of the background, an accompaniment to the business at hand.

The gentle plunk of a rise further upstream prompted me to look up from drifting the nymph, and as I watched, a few other trout took up stations and began to rise along the edge of a cutbank. Another good thing about fishing in May is that the trout are very businesslike. When the bugs hatch, the trout rise.

After working through several fly changes without a take, I finally switched to a tiny Pheasant Tail Nymph and picked off a fat trout on the next drift. It was the first good trout of the new season, deep, thick, and fully recovered from last fall's spawning, its large dark spots surrounded by bright halos, a splash of yellow along its flanks.

The trout's run upstream had put down the others, so I backed away from the stream and waited for things to settle down. As I sat, the calls of the warblers and whitethroats moved once again into the foreground, along with the murmur of the current. I saw another redstart flashing through the bushes and was reminded why they are called *candelitas* "little candles" in Mexico.

Sitting there and listening , I saw another angler walking up the opposite bank. He stopped, looked intently at the water, made a few casts, and continued upstream toward me. He was well tricked out—waders, a vest with many fly boxes and club patches. Polaroid glasses, a tweed hat—every inch an expert, by the look of him. I might have called out "Any luck?" but I didn't want to distract him. So I kept still and watched as he came closer.

Then I noticed that he had earphones in his ears. Their cords joined below his chin and led to a tape player stuffed into a large pocked on this vest. He stopped, stepped quietly into the tail of the pool below me, and began to work upstream, making short, accurate casts under the edges of the alders.

I tried to imagine what he could be listening to. Classical music, perhaps—Schubert's "Trout Quintet" came to mind, or "The Moldau" by Smetana. Or maybe a Mozart piano sonata, to match the elegance of his casting.

He didn't look the type to be listening to show tunes or country-western music, although modern jazz might be a possibility. Maybe he wasn't listening to music at all—perhaps a recording of John Gierach reading from *Trout Bum,* or a self-improvement program on how to plan for retirement.

Whatever it was, it didn't distract him from his fishing. I saw his rod lift to a good fish, which he netted and returned very efficiently, with none of my usual fumbling. As he looked up from releasing the trout, he saw me crouching there upstream. I raised a hand and pointed to the pool above me.

He smiled, nodded, and began a wide circle away from the bank so he would not disturb the fish I was working. The last I saw of him was his tweedy hat and the shiny metal band of the earphones, moving just above the brush. The birds, hushed as he moved through the thicket, began to sing again. Soon the trout began to rise, and the music faded into the background once again as I moved up to cast.

VI

Traditions

Classic Water

The spring creek wound its way back and forth across the fresh green meadow, its smooth, almost oily surface shielded by the waving grasses along the bank, its current swirling soundlessly through the braided channels in the weeds. The meadow reached eastward to the rolling wooded hills, and the scene was completed by a newly painted red barn and clean white farmhouse. I heard a rooster crow in celebration, and a meadowlark answered from atop a fencepost.

If there ever was "classic water" in the English dry fly tradition, I thought, this is it, and as if to affirm the similarity, a brown trout rose along a current seam. Kneeling on the bank near the tail of the pool, I looked down to make sure my fly line wasn't tangled in the stems or caught under my knees. But just as I made ready to cast, a redwinged blackbird flew across my line of sight and over the rising fish, and the answering boil and push over the weeds told me the trout had spooked out of its feeding lane to an undercut along the far bank.

I said something inelegant, but because the trout was a good one (I had glimpsed its bronzy flanks), I decided to wait and see if it would come out again. A sparse hatch of tiny Blue-winged Olives was coming off, one of the classic hatches of the western Wisconsin spring creeks, and I could see other, smaller rises further upstream. I told myself I would rather hook up on one good fish than play tag with the little ones. Besides, this looked like a perfect setup.

In preparation for the trout's return, I made a couple of casts to get the drift just right, so that the tiny fly would float down without drag—not so easy with the current coiling through the weedbeds and the intermittent wind whisking across the surface. But the light four-weight fly rod was made for this sort of work, and I was hopeful of success.

As I sat back in the grass to wait, I looked down at my equipment again. There in a setting that Skues or Halford or even Izaak Walton's fly-fishing friend Charles Cotton would find familiar, I realized that almost nothing of my tackle fit the "classic" tradition. My fly rod was made of graphite fiber, not split bamboo, and my fly line was the latest synthetic high floater, not enameled silk. My leader was nylon monofilament, not silkworm gut, and even the fly was completely outside the tradition—tied on a chemically sharpened hook, its tail of Microfibbett fibers, body of synthetic fur dubbing, polypropylene wing, and pre-waxed nylon thread. Even the hackle was "genetic blue dun," smacking of white lab coats and artificial gene manipulation rather than a blue-grey Andalusian rooster strutting in the farmyard. Plastic Polaroid glasses, recycled fiber vest, neoprene waders, synthetic leather wading shoes, Gore-Tex rain parka, Supplex shirt—it seemed that everything I had was made of unpronounceable molecules existing nowhere in nature, and I felt a momentary qualm.

A few years ago I read an article about a Pennsylvania angler who fished exclusively with antique equipment and built his own greenheart rods, made his own horsehair line and leaders, formed his hooks from heated needles, and used only natural materials in his flies. I knew "Natural or synthetic?" was becoming a frequent question in fly-tying shops, like "Paper or plastic?" in the supermarket. New builders of traditional split cane rods had emerged and some were doing a thriving business. Antique bamboo rods were commanding high prices—even rods once sold by Sears and Western Auto stores. Perhaps others were feeling similar qualms.

As I watched the water, I recalled another "classic" situation many years earlier, when I fished the Junction Pool where Willowemoc Creek, joins the storied Beaverkill—an eastern Mecca in the Catskills tradition, the birthplace of fly fishing in America. No one could fault my obedience to tradition then, for in the spirit of the place, I was using a split bamboo rod, and HDH silk fly line, a size #14 Quill Gordon tied in the best Eastern style—even a gut leader I had carefully saved. It would be easy enough to romanticize the occasion—indeed, I had done so already through my choice of tackle.

But the silk line would sink at just the wrong moment, despite having enough Mucilin on it to float a grindstone, and the gut leader, though carefully soaked in the best tradition, was stiff and unreliable—4X gut was less than two-pound test, and finger gut was almost unobtainable. Despite these travails, I did manage to catch a lovely 14-inch brown trout, making my pilgrimage worthwhile. Were it not for the notes in my fishing journal, I would almost surely have forgotten how I struggled with the gut leader and how vehemently I had cursed that wretched silk line.

The plunk of a rise brought me quickly back to the present situation. The brown trout had moved back to its feeding lane, and the blue-winged olives continued to float here and there down the smooth surface like a regatta of miniature sailboats. I slowly rose up to my knees, rolled the line forward, made two false casts with the crisp little graphite rod, and dropped the tiny dry fly a few feet above the rise. Despite the twisting currents, the fly line floated down perfectly, the long fine leader—thinner and stronger than any silkworm gut—lay almost invisible on the surface with just the right amount of slack, and the dry fly floated perkily on its genetic hackles and synthetic fiber tails. For me it was a rare moment—a perfect cast and a dragless float to a classic rise.

"So much for tradition," I said aloud. And as if to punctuate that remark, the trout rose and took the fly.

The Fly Book

The spring woods were still damp from the meltwater, and green shoots were just beginning to push through the sodden brown leaves carpeting the forest floor. To the south, the trees were leafing out and flowers were in bloom, but a late spring had left northern Wisconsin far behind. Except for a few buds and spikes of fresh green here and there, it looked like November.

The fishing was far behind too. I had invested most of a day on the river, more as gesture than anything. The water was cold, and very little bug life had shown. It really was a day for drifting nightcrawlers into deep holes, but my chenille version of a redworm had drawn little interest.

As I plodded back to the pickup, I told myself the trip had been worth it just to get away from the office, but I wasn't very convincing, and I walked along head down in obvious defeat. Then I chanced to see an old leather fly book just beside the trail, half covered by moldering leaves.

I stopped and picked it up. The leather was black and cracked from alternately drying and getting wet again, and the underside was damp and slimy in my hand. The zipper was rusted shut, and no doubt the flies it contained were ruined, but I took it along anyway.

Back at the truck, it took a little oil and some work to get the zipper unstuck. Finally I got it moving and unzipped the fly book inch by inch. It was so discolored from the dampness that I couldn't tell how old it was, but I knew such fly books were common a generation or two ago.

I spread open the sheared lamb's wool and found it only slightly damp inside. As I expected, everything was rusted, and there were ochre stains on the creamy wool, but the hooks had not yet crumbled, and most of the flies were at least recognizable.

Several of the flies were very old, probably plucked from a Weber display card in a hardware store. They were tied with dyed duck quill wings in a style long since vanished—a Yellow Sally, a Red Ibis, a Professor, a Black Gnat, a McGinty, a Grizzly King, and others I couldn't name. The Yellow Sally was tied on a Sneck hook which had almost square bend—something I had never seen outside old fishing books and tackle catalogs from the 1940's.

There were also several flyrod-size lures, common before the advent of spinning tackle: a tiny orange and black Flatfish with a single hook, several spinner-fly combinations, a couple of Colorado spinners, and three Beetle Bugs—round metal lures painted to look like ladybird beetles, with a small fringe of dark hair glued underneath.

My uncle was part of this generation of fly fishermen—a generation who worked hard and never threw anything away—and his fly boxes contained several old, heavily-tied wet flies of the same style, along with a few spinner-fly combinations and the inevitable Colorado spinners. They looked impossibly clunky next to the tiny emergers, no-hackles, and wispy Catskill-style flies I had come to favor.

But flies like these were with me when I began fly-fishing for trout many years ago. No doubt in response to an incessant stream of questions about flies and fly-fishing, my uncle sent me a small plastic box of flies from Von

Lengerek & Antoine in Chicago—among them a Sure Strike Special, sort of a Coachman Trude with red floss ribbing over the peacock herl body. The other flies were a heavily tied McGinty with a thick squirrel-hair wing, a bushy Gray Hackle Peacock, and a red and white Parmacheene Belle.

It was 1953, late May, and the banks of the river near our home were still brown and redolent with the smell of damp earth and rotting leaves. There I had caught many chubs and suckers on worms and a few small northern pike and two large brown trout on Daredevil spoons. But now I had my father's long white Shakespeare fly rod, and ancient "Expert" fly reel, a cheap nylon fly line, some sort of tapered leader—and I was really trout fishing.

Instead of soaking a worm or heaving a spoon in the slow pool where we used to swim in summer, I moved upstream to the quick water coming in. There, just like it said in Ray Bergman's book, a trout was rising at the edge of the current. Opening my brand-new VL&A box, I picked out the Sure Strike Special and tied it to the leader.

My casting style had also been learned from a book and looked it, but I did manage several floats over the rising trout. Then the dart and clatter of a kingfisher caught my eyes and the fly drifted down, and I glanced away for an instant. When I looked back, the perky white wing of the fly was gone. I tightened, and a brown trout of surprising power bolted out of the run and into the deep amber water of the big pool. The heavy fly rod was almost an insult to his strength, but I drew the fish in and finally scooped it up in awkward triumph—a 14-inch brown trout, my first on a fly.

I remembered all this and much more as I poked through the matted hackles of the flies in the old leather fly book, wishing I could breathe some life back into them. There was no name, no way to find its owner. None of the flies or lures was in fishable condition, and rust had eaten its way into everything.

Still, I couldn't bring myself to throw it away, so I walked back down the trail and left it atop a bare rock. The man who lost it might return—or perhaps another angler would spread it open and be flooded with memories of his own.

Hair Bugs and Stump-Knockers

It may be that too much delicacy and finesse can blunt the basic instincts of fishing. Fussing with 7X tippets and tiny flies seems almost to remove fishing entirely from its hunter-gatherer origins. I enjoy it, but I also like tossing a plug at a hole in the lily pads or bouncing a big hair bug off a log, hoping that a largemouth bass will come up and try to tear it apart.

With this in mind I visited a small lake in early summer, before the weeds had grown up too thick. I arrived just before dawn and launched my canoe into the mist as the robins were tuning up. My gear was simple—a fly rod, a plugcasting rod, some hair bugs and poppers, and a few old bass lures.

I paddled across the lake (don't we all?) and set up at the mouth of a small bay. Glossy lily pads were spread among a dozen gray and battered stumps and sunken logs. The bay smelled of life and of decay. As I anchored the canoe within casting range of several likely targets, a green frog jumped into the dark water and scrambled back up on the end of a half-sunk log.

A great blue heron patrolled the far end of the bay, moving with infinite slowness and unmistakable intensity. I rigged up the fly rod with a brown and white hair bug, then set up the casting rod with what my father called a "stump-knocker," a cigar-shaped wooden plug. Its painted frog-finish was cracked and chipped. A black and green dragonfly lighted on the thwart, brushed off its see-everything eyes, and darted away.

I stood up, stripped off some fly line, made a couple of false casts, and dropped the hair bug next to one of the stumps. I jiggled the bug a little, then let it sit, my rod pointing straight down the line. I found myself hunching over like the heron, waiting and watching. I tried to visualize a tough old largemouth looking up at the bug. After a full minute, I twitched it again. Its feathery business end wiggled in the water, and its deerhair head floated awash.

No takers, so I swam the bug to the edge of a lily pad and bumped it as if it were trying to climb aboard. That was convincing—the water churned and the bug vanished. I tightened up and skulldragged the bass out of the weeds, stripping hard to bring it close, and had it lipped and out of the water in another minute—a three-pounder, its tail still red from spawning.

As I slipped the fish back, the heron crouched down and took wing, flapping slowly along the shoreline and around the point. The sun was well up now, and water striders skated from pad to pad. The glowing clouds of mist began to move out across the water. I cast the bug toward another stump.

This time I overshot, but the bug had a weedguard and didn't hang up. I crept it slowly forward until if fell off the stump. Once again I straightened the fly line and let the bug just sit there, not quite still. It almost seemed to be moving of its own accord. But nothing came after it.

Nobody home at this hole, I thought, so I stripped in the bug, laid down the fly rod, and picked up the casting rod with the stump-knocker plug. I cast the big plug into open water behind me a few times to warm up, then turned and cast to a dark slot among the lily pads.

Long ago I had learned to wait until the ripples subsided before moving a surface plug, so once again I found myself in the familiar heron-like posture. After a few moments, I reeled up a little slack and "nodded" the plug, just enough to make a few ripples.

After the third or fourth nod a half-pounder nailed it. The little bass must have felt very brave to try to eat a plug almost half as long as he was. I cast again and brought the plug in a slow zig-zag past another stump. It didn't get far, and soon I released a bigger fish, about two pounds.

After all the ruckus subsided, I lifted the anchor and let the canoe drift further down the edge of the weedbed. Then I went back to the fly rod and the old hair bug. Two more largemouths ate the bug in short order. The old instincts were on full alert now, and I felt good about the morning.

Then, as I straightened up to make another cast, I heard a high-pitched whine. Two jet-skis blasted around the point and ran past me, each driver in a purple and chartreuse vest. I had to sit down in the canoe as their wakes washed through the weedbed.

One of the jet-skis turned back and swung in closer to me. The rider had a long ponytail and a bright red sunburn. He waved and shouted "How's the fishin?" as he pitched in his own wake. I shrugged and pointed to my ear, pretending I couldn't hear him.

He looked me over, waved and roared away across the lake. Minutes later he and his companion were back, blowing past me and waving again. It was nearly nine o'clock, and I soon heard the roar of other boats. Then a sparkling maroon bass boat came racing across the water, and I was soon joined by two men in matching red gimme caps. They also waved, opened suitcase-size tackle boxes, and began to rig up.

My notions of reawakening old instincts now seemed a bit quaint, and I felt out of place with my old-fashioned hair bugs and wooden plugs. I cast again, but the energy had gone out of the morning. A few minutes later, I began to paddle back across the lake.

On the way, I waved to the passing boats. It seemed the thing to do.

Lunch Break

It had been a busy morning, with a good hatch of straw-colored caddisflies and several eager rises. But now the sun was bright overhead, and the chorus of birds that greeted the dawn was quiet in the midday heat. The aspen leaves twisted and turned high above my head, but no breath of wind ruffled the surface of the big pool.

A good time for lunch, I thought. A favorite log lay just upstream near the head of the pool, so I waded ashore and pushed through the streamside brush until I reached a shattered stump, broken off in some long-ago storm. Fingers of dry wood still thrust upward like a warning hand, while the trunk lay half buried in the undergrowth.

Years ago, part of my lunchtime ritual was to dip some water from the stream, but fears of giardiasis and human contamination had long since persuaded me to bring my own drinking water. The cool creek water tumbling down the rapids looked very inviting compared to the warm tap water in my flask, but there was no help for it.

I leaned my fly rod against a moose maple, sat down on the ancient log, pulled out my lunch bag and a folding knife, and began to unwrap a chunk of cheese, glossy yellow like the buttercups clustered in the sun along the bank. Another package held a thick slice of French bread and a plastic envelope of mustard, and another a shiny green Granny Smith apple.

With deliberate strokes I sliced the cheese and quartered the apple. Keeping one eye on the apple, I folded half of the French bread over three slices of cheese, daubed on some mustard, and took a big, satisfying bite. The sunlight sparkled in the rapids above the pool, and I could feel its heat through my waders.

Right on cue, a chipmunk appeared, wary of any sudden movement. Apparently it had grown accustomed to sharing lunch with fishermen, for it hopped boldly up onto the log, whiskers trembling, and peered intently at the remaining bread and cheese.

I pinched off a bit of bread from my sandwich and tossed it to the chipmunk, it darted away a foot or so, then came back inch by inch and finally seized the bread. Then it vanished into the leafy undergrowth, only to return a few moments later. By then I had placed several bits of bread and cheese a safe distance away, so the chipmunk could come and go at will.

I decided the sun was a bit too warm and shuffled down the log a little further, into the shade, but where I could still see the river. As I ate my bread and cheese and watched the pool, I was reminded of another lunch with a friend, now gone, who took special delight in food --more, I suspect, than he did in fishing. At a time when I clanked and jingled like a tinker with a myriad of clippers, forceps, magnifiers and fly boxes, his vest and battered willow creel were filled with goodies, leaving barely enough room for a couple of fly boxes and a few spools of leader material.

Once we met at a favorite rock just above a small waterfall. My lunch was a mashed-down peanut butter sandwich and a dill pickle, but when I started to unwrap it, he waved the bag aside, offered a piece of salmon, and said "Put that away and try this!" As I gratefully munched the salmon, he opened his creel and pulled out two celery stalks, a green onion, a plastic bag of cooked flaked trout, a squeeze bottle of mayonnaise, and a jar of Dijon mustard. Then he produced two enormous Kaiser rolls and a bag of freshly-picked watercress, and before long I had a trout salad sandwich in hand.

"Now, just wait," he said and he scrambled down the rocky slope, returning moments later with a dripping half bottle of Chardonnay he had stashed in the river. "The wine should be chilled just right," he proclaimed, flourishing a corkscrew from a pocket in his vest. And as if all this were not enough, he reached into his creel yet again and extracted two maroon and gold peaches for dessert.

"What's the occasion?" I asked, sucking the last of the sweet pulp from my peach pit.

"This is it," he replied, his sweeping gesture taking in the river, the sparkling waterfall, the ferns dappled with spots of sunlight. And he was right—there was more than enough to celebrate.

We fished together another time, a blustery day on another river reputed to hold an autumn steelhead run. After a fishless morning that left us wet and shivering, he came to the rescue with crackers, cheese, and a thermos of hot chili. As he heated water in the tea pail over a smoky fire, I fiddled with my tackle, looking forward to some tea, only to find hot buttered rum in my cup, complete with a lemon slice and cinnamon stick. We didn't catch any-thing that day, but I can still taste the chili and the rum after all these years.

Remembering those splendid lunch breaks, my simple bread and cheese and fruit seemed almost Spartan, although the chipmunk was happy with it and began nosing closer, looking for more crumbs. As I watched the river, it seemed that I could recall almost every lunch break, many alone, some with friends—like the first meal of fresh deer liver and onions at the hunt-ing shack, or the bright campfires that punctuate a canoe trip.

The rise of a small trout in the middle of the pool brought me back to the present. The chipmunk had cleaned up the remnant of the bread and cheese, and the mice or the ants would surely find the apple core I tossed into the undergrowth. I stood up, stuffed the empty lunch bag into the back pocket of my vest, and lifted my flask to celebrate the occasion.

The Outsider

On a cold January afternoon I headed west to a large and heavily fished lake, well known for good ice fishing. I hadn't fished there in the winter be-fore, but I had a detailed contour map and some advice from the bait shop owner to show me where to go.

Arriving at the landing, I loaded up my toboggan with my Finnish auger, a foam plastic bucket with a few minnows, a jigging rod, a box of lures and bobbers, an ice skimmer, and a bucket to sit on—all pretty simple. It was the same outfit I used when I started fishing "hard water" in Minnesota years before. I was new to Wisconsin at the time, so I didn't know much about tipups and ice shanties—and I still don't. Then I checked the map, buttoned up my down-filled parka, and set off across the ice.

The snow crunched under my packs, the toboggan squeaked in the cold, and swirls of powdery snow raced high over the lake like dust-devils on summer prairies. I followed a well-worn track through a village of ice shanties. There were pickup trucks and snowmobiles everywhere, but no people. Then a red flag popped upright, a door opened, and two men in blaze orange caps ran to the tipup. One of them lifted it out, hauled a few times, and yanked a small northern pike out on the ice. They rebaited their tipup, set it over the hole, and disappeared back into their shanty.

I plodded further down the lake. I was not surprised at the number of shanties, but I soon realized the "shanty" was a misnomer. As I passed one, the door opened and I glimpsed a card table, a portable television, and a man holding a steaming coffeepot—all the comforts of home. Some shanties even had curtains on the windows. I half expected to see window boxes and plastic geraniums.

Distracted by the hard-packed trail, I had to recheck my compass and relate the shoreline to the contour map to figure out my position. I walked another hundred yards, ignoring the tire tracks and snowmobile paths this time.

Finally I was close to where the map indicated a dropoff and a deep slot that connected to a mid-lake channel. There were only a few shanties nearby, and I saw a face appear momentarily at a window. I untied the auger and drilled a hole, found it was too shallow, and moved another fifty paces north before drilling again. On the third try I found good depth and clean bottom, so I drilled two more holes close by. I took off my heavy parka after drilling the second hole, but with the wind whispering insistently down the lake, driving puffs of powder ahead of it, I soon had it on again.

I cleared the slush from the hole, rigged my jigging rod with a Swedish Pimple, hooked on a minnow head freshly pinched off, and began to work it in small lifts and drops a foot or two off the bottom. Sometimes I reached forward and dropped the lure all the way to the bottom to kick up a puff of silt—a deadly line move, at least in Minnesota. But I often just let the lure hang, rotating back and forth from the twists in the line, never quite motionless.

I looked up from time to time, half expecting to see a timber wolf trotting across the frozen lake, as I had the year before, when I snowshoed in to fish the trout lakes of the Gunflint Trail. It was almost as cold, but the rows of summer cottages and the whine of a racing snowmobile dispelled any such illusions.

As the wind picked up in the late afternoon, I pulled my fur-edged hood over my head, half covering my face, and gradually the universe constricted down to my little hole in the ice and the imagined flutterings of the lure. For a long time nothing took hold, but just when I thought I would move to another hole, the rod tip bent down and I set the hook in a small pike, which I released. It was too early for the walleyes to be moving.

Sitting there with the snow rustling around my boots, I remembered another day on another lake, far to the north, and the company of an old friend. In those days, I would try to get a week off in early February to fish for lake trout, and always worked in a day or two with Claude, who lived across the highway from our cabin on Lake Superior.

Claude was in his late 70's then, hard of hearing and stooped from years of toil in his garden, but tough and gentle—a good combination of strength and temperament when he worked as a foreman in the CCC camps. After we drilled our holes and baited our lines, Claude would relive those days and many others with stories of fighting fire, bushwhacking many miles to find beaver ponds full of brook trout, chasing bears out of the cook shack, and so on. Though I had heard all the stories many times, it was good to hear them again and see his weatherbeaten face light up with the memories.

Tipups were not legal in Minnesota in those days, but we would place a twig near each hole and drape the line loosely over the branches. When a trout took the bait, the twig would bounce and sometimes even be pulled into the hole.

Claude believed wholeheartedly in minnows, usually fishing two on a hook for extra action. He shook his head and smiled doubtfully when I showed him a Finnish jigging lure that looked a lot like a small cisco. It swooped invitingly in wide circles when lifted and dropped. He could hardly believe it when I hooked a large trout on it—only to break it off in the hole after an abortive stab with the gaff. I could see that big head dropping back down the hole into the dark water, with the lure still stuck in its nose. . .

"What are you doin' out here by yourself?" I turned, startled out of my recollections, as footsteps crunched close behind me. I peered through the frosty wolf fur of my hood. A shanty fisherman stood there, silhouetted against the fading sunlight in the west. As I looked around, he put down his minnow bucket, shivered, and rubbed his arms.

With all the shanties around me, I was hardly alone, but I was the only fisherman sitting outside, so I guess I was by myself in a way. I replied that I was just hoping to pick up a walleye. Besides, I said, I liked to feel the fish take hold.

"A walleye!" he snorted. "You'll wait a long time to get a walleye outa this lake. What are you using?"

I reeled up my jigging outfit and showed him the Swedish Pimple. He snorted again and shook his head. I asked him how he was doing, and he said they had caught several northern pike "big enough to pickle." He left then and trudged back to his shanty, while I dropped the lure back in the hole to resume its dance.

As the gray afternoon light faded into evening, people began to leave, and the ice boomed and cracked ominously as they drove by. Some passed close and slowed down to look me over, and I realized I must be something of an oddity sitting out on the ice in my fur ruff and iced-up beard.

Watching the last of them go, I almost forgot the lure dangling in the dark water, but I struck instinctively at a soft tug. The reel chattered as the rod doubled, and I had a busy few minutes before I had a fish in the hole. A quick grab and it was on the ice—a two-pound walleye, dark-backed and flecked with gold and blue, clean and hard like all winter fish.

Quickly rebaiting with a fresh minnow head, I dropped the Pimple back in the hole, touched the bottom, reeled up a few turns, and felt another thump. A few minutes later I had another walleye on the ice, bigger than the first.

Hoping I hadn't attracted any more attention from the departing pickup trucks and snowmobiles, I dropped the Pimple down again. It took longer this time, but soon another walleye had it. This one was lightly hooked, so I turned it back, watching its white-tipped tail disappear into the darkness.

Night was coming on quickly now, so I reeled up, put my snow-encrusted fish in a gunnysack, and began the long trek back to the landing. The toboggan creaked in the cold, and the snow continued to whisper around the abandoned shanties.

The stars were out when I slid the old and battered toboggan into the truck, slammed the tailgate, and cranked the cold engine. As I left the landing and passed a brightly lit cafe, I was suddenly hungry, so I pulled over, sloughed off my big parka and its still frosty ruff, walked in and sat down in a booth.

Wiping the fog from my glasses, I couldn't help overhearing voices from a nearby booth. One was laughing, "Yeah, this little guy was all alone, in a big fur parka, like, from the Yoo-kon, ya know. And all he had was a jig pole and some kinda spoon. 'Fishing for walleyes,' he said! Har, har! Bet he froze his butt off!" Other voices joined in the laughter.

I smiled at the menu as the frost in my beard began to melt.

The Old Man and the Flute

Thomas Wolfe is known, among other things, for the saying, "You can't go home again." I usually take that expression to heart, because when I have gone back to visit streams or lakes I knew as a boy, they are invariably disappointing. The faint trail in the woods has become a bicycle path; a once pristine shoreline is crowded with summer homes; the moccasin flowers and Jack-in-the pulpits have disappeared.

So it was with some anxiety that I returned to a steam I had fished often as a boy but hadn't seen for many years. This time I didn't exactly go alone: I was accompanied by a cloud of recollections of the old man who fished there with me.

The steam was enclosed in tall grass—that much was still the same—but it seemed narrower and smaller than I remembered. The current murmured secretively, and the curved banks were undercut—inviting hidey-holes for big brown trout. I hadn't brought a rod; I just wanted to see it all again.

When I walked around a stand of alders and scrub and saw the old maple tree, the flood of memories was almost too much. The old man and I would meet there after the morning's fishing and eat our lunch, talk a little, and fiddle with our tackle. I walked over and sat down in our accustomed spot, where we used to watch the big pool.

The old man could no longer tie his own flies (or, as he said it, "flice), and he liked my bushy, crudely overdressed dry flies. The last time we fished together, he called me at home the night before, and like so many old people of that era, shouted into the telephone as if I were across the continent instead of a few miles down the road. "Yust bring some a dem yellow and brown ones," he said.

I recalled the long, dusty drive to the railroad crossing and the awkward walk through the grassy hummocks to the stream—tough for me, much tougher for him. We would separate as usual after stashing a couple of cans of beer in the water. From long habit, we said very little.

He know the stream so well that he could walk from one dark undercut to another, creep up quietly, and dap his fly in the water without showing himself. If nothing took hold, he would sometimes spit on the fly, mash it down a bit, and fish it sunk. I couldn't imagine what it looked like to the fish—maybe a grasshopper, but more likely just a bug down on its luck.

As I sat against the old tree, I remembered our last lunch. We each had a bologna sandwich, a pickle, a couple of store-bought cookies, and a peach—

plus the beer, of course. (I don't think his wife allowed beer at home, but I wouldn't dare say anything about it –anyway, I was too young to have beer.) Our fish bags lay in the shade, and I could see that his held several hefty trout. It had that sweet smell of fresh trout and damp ferns.

We sat and watched the stream for a long time, eating slowly while the bees grumbled in the goldenrod and a kingfisher rattled its way across the pool. A whitethroat whistled once in the midday heat, then was silent. Then the old man reached into his jacket and pulled out a black leatherette case, and from another pocket a folded piece of paper. It was a piece of sheet music, and it had been folded and unfolded many times. He carefully opened the case, and the blue velvet inside was incongruously bright in the sun. His gnarled and knobby hands with the big knuckles trembled as he fitted together an old flute. I could see where the silver plating had worn through to the brass underneath.

He placed a stick on the sheet music to hold it flat and, without a word, he began to play. I recognized the tune, although I didn't know its name. I had heard the cooks at school singing it in the kitchen as they worked. He played for several minutes, and I noticed he was no longer looking at the sheet music. It seemed that everything else had become quiet, listening while he played. I sat and listened, not knowing what to say or do.

My half empty beer can was warm when he stopped playing, folded up the sheet music, and carefully put away the old flute, still without a word. Then he looked up and said, "Vell, dere's more trout in the crick. Let's go visit dem." I didn't know then that this would be our last trip together, but maybe he did.

As I sat under the maple, I could see it all again, and though it was many years ago, I could still hum snatches of that old song. The bees droned in the goldenrod as they had before, and a small trout rose bravely in the middle of the pool. I got up and stumbled back over the hummocky ground and down the railroad grade to the car.

Going home again can be hard.

The Tackle Box

Last year I had the hard task of going through my father's belongings. He had lived long and actively, and he was of that generation who grew up poor, survived the Depression and never threw anything away. It was left for us to rummage through boxes and boxes of papers, old photographs, magazines, coils of wire, vacuum tubes, jars of screws, and spare parts for hundreds of home-made gadgets and discarded appliances.

He hadn't fished much since moving east, which surprised me, since he was a serious bass fisherman, and there was good fishing to be had in New Jersey. But he felt very much out of his element there, and he seemed to have turned a page in his life when he was transferred.

I found his old tackle box in a cluttered corner of the crawlspace, tucked under an antique Shaker chair, and the dust lay thick upon it. The latch never worked right, and it was held tight with a large safety-pin. Nearby was the Army surplus ammunition box with the tools he used when the 4.2 horsepower Johnson outboard needed work.

I knelt down and opened the tackle box, knowing there would be a flood of memories from my boyhood. I still had a few of his "stump-knocker" bass plugs, but there would be other lures in that box, cracked and gouged from hard use.

In the top tray were three Heddon River Runts, two floaters and a sinker, red and white. This was our daytime standard for bass and pike, and I caught my first bass on one. I recalled the somewhat stagy Huck Finn photograph—a three-year old boy in corduroy overalls, T-shirt and straw hat, holding up his first big fish—a picture of my father kept in his wallet for 50 years. When I first started, he would cast and I would reel in the plug. When the bass took hold, I just kept reeling as hard as I could, burning my thumb and barking some skin off my knuckles.

In the bottom of the box was the very reel I used that day—a Shakespeare "Criterion" level-wind with jeweled bearings and ivory handles. It felt familiar, for I had picked many backlashes from it while learning to cast. That reel used to be clamped to a five-foot solid rapier-steel rod made by American Fork & Hoe, later to become True Temper, with ruby-red agate guides. In those days we carried only this bait-casting outfit and used it for everything—bass, walleyes, northern pike, and muskies. The next tray held two Arbogast Jitterbugs, a wooden Creek Chub Plunker, a Johnson Silver Minnow, a Lazy Ike, a chewed-up Mud Puppy, and a fuzzy gray Heddon Crazy Crawler. We used the Silver Minnow or the frog-finish Plunker for bass in daylight, the Lazy Ike for walleyes, and the Mud Puppy or the Crazy Crawler for muskies. The Jitterbug was the only plug we used at night, when we got serious about bass fishing.

I remembered the night we caught six bass over four pounds (two were over five) in a lake near home. In those days, we rented a wooden boat from a farmer, always remembering to ask him to turn off the dock light after the last boat had come in. The darker the night the better—we never went out on moonlit nights.

I would fish until after sundown, then I took over the oars while he stood in the stern. He greased the oarlocks so they wouldn't squeak, and then we would row down the dark shoreline. "Hard on the left," he'd say, and I would pull the left oar one time. "Hard on both of'em," and we glided silently forward. "Let it drift," and we listened for the sound of a feeding fish. All the while he would cast the Jitterbug and wring every ounce of temptation from each retrieve.

Depending on the size of the boat we rented, I could be sitting pretty close to him as he cast. At night we didn't fool with the landing net. Instead, he landed bass by reeling them up short and using their own speed in the water to boost them up and over the gunwale. That night my knees were sideswiped several times as bass were swung into the boat, but we didn't lose a one. We traded places in the boat—a sure sign of a successful night—and I caught another four-pounder within yards of the landing.

Shortly after midnight we beached the battered old boat, placed the stringer in a washtub in the trunk of our old 1939 Mercury, covered the fish with a wet gunnysack, and drove home. Mom was awake, waiting up as usual, with a box of Wheaties, a bottle of milk, and two bowls on the kitchen table. Usually we just carried the stringer down to the creek behind the house, but this time I carried it inside, barely able to keep from dragging the fish, to show her what we had caught. How she smiled and clapped her hands in amazement at what her men had brought home, and how proud she was when I pointed out the one I had caught near the boat dock just before midnight.

The next few compartments held the "interior decorator" lures, the baits we almost never used. There was a Paul Bunyan "66", its feathers long since turned to dust, and next to it an Arbogast Hawaiian Wiggler, its rubber skirts dried up and stuck to the bottom of the tray. Next were some June Bug spinners, a snarl of leaders, a tube of reel oil, and an empty bottle of 6-12 bug dope.

In the bottom of the box was a rusted Langley De-Liar scale, a pair of long-nose pliers, a spool of Shakespeare "Wexford" 15-pound black casting line, a scaler, a dried-up jar of Uncle Josh pork frogs, a tube of grease, an extra starter cord and spark plugs for the outboard, and a crumbling cork stuck full of bait hooks. My father said a boy couldn't learn to fish right with a bobber, so I always fished "tight line" with a light cane pole, line, and hook when we went after bluegills or perch.

I remembered being corroded with envy when he took my brother fishing one morning at the North Woods Club and came back with a dozen large bluegills, splendidly orange-breasted, their combined weight just under nine pounds. In those days we had the "two hands rule"—we could keep no bluegills smaller than our two hands put together. Otherwise, the screened live box at the dock would have been full of sunfish.

My long silence in the crawlspace finally attracted attention, and my wife called to me to ask about yet another folder of documents upstairs. Most of the tackle was rusted or corroded beyond use. I saved out the Shakespeare "criterion" reel and after looking over the contents closed the box one last time.

The Rotation

The Margaree was behaving just like a spate river is supposed to. A week before we arrived on Cape Breton Island, rains in the high country had raised the water level three feet. The river had begun to drop toward normal level, but more rain was expected any day. Heavy clouds and wind-swept fog were typical conditions for a good run, but so far only a few salmon had been seen.

The rise in the water level encouraged everyone at Brown's Inn. It might bring on a fresh run of late fall salmon, more likely to take a fly than the stale fish that held in the named pools and were growing darker every day. The pools I had fished for two weeks the year before were no longer low and clear--they were swift and off color just enough to make wading difficult.

These conditions were strange to me. I was even more conscious of the slippery "rolly rocks" in the stream bed. I decided it was safer to fish water I had seen before. Earlier in the morning I fished through the Wash Pool and the Doyle Pool, swinging a large black and purple marabou Spey fly with a traditional 14-foot Spey rod, but I came up empty.

I decided to drive back to Brown's Inn near Margaree Center and get some advice from John Brown. John had grown up on Cape Breton Island and spent most of his adult life on or near the river. On our first visit he had shown me where the high water had reached--about ten feet over my head–and how the river reshaped itself anew every year. I had been lucky that year--a salmon caught and released the first day, then a grilse a few days later, both dark fish, with coloring very like a brown trout. This year I had fished nine days without raising a fish, and this was starting to look like the tenth. Only one angler at Brown's Inn had hooked more than one fish in the days since our arrival.

On my way back to the inn I passed the Margaree Salmon Museum, where I had spent several hours admiring the flies, rods, and reels of the past. The displays included a working model of the Margaree watershed, including more than forty named pools. I had thought about checking with the curator, who had a great love for her museum and seemed to know just about everything that was going on in the valley, but I continued on. I clattered onto the one-lane bridge over the Cranton Pool, the last before Margaree Centre.

No one was fishing the pool, but something about it looked good--good enough for me to pull off the road into the parking area. Another car arrived as I was getting out. The driver was tall, athletic despite his years. He looked every inch an experienced salmon angler. We chatted for a few minutes as we rigged up. I mentioned that this was my second trip to the Margaree, probably hoping for some free advice. He told me he had fished the Margaree for 28 years, in good times and bad. Whatever his luck had been in the past, he said he had not seen a single salmon since he arrived ten days ago. After a few more minutes I waved him on the river while I tied on a fresh black and purple marabou fly.

He walked down the steep gravel slope to the river. The rocks of the shingle were slick and wobbly, but he waded easily without a staff, casting across and downstream, swinging the fly until it hung straight downstream. He would hold it there for half a minute, then lift the line in a powerful back cast, let it unroll, then shoot the forward cast across and downstream. The cast lay straight, fishing immediately as it began to swing across the current. Then he took three or four steps downstream as he tracked the fly's position with his rod tip.

I admired the efficiency of his casting. Once he had reached his optimum length, the timing of his casting stroke never varied as he moved further down the pool. I stayed a good distance behind him, ever mindful of the ethics of the rotation. I had encountered the rotation system several times on my first visit, especially at the Snag Pool and the Long Pool, where we were often ten or more anglers spread along their considerable lengths.

The rotation is a tradition with almost the force of law. The first angler to arrive at a pool enters near the head and starts fishing. The next angler to arrive waits until the first angler has moved far enough downstream (about a cast and a half), and then he begins casting in the same manner, across and downstream. Subsequent anglers continue the pattern. The first angler usually gets out of the pool near the tailout and walks back upstream to fish it through again. Several pools have white painted benches or plastic lawn chairs where the anglers can sit and talk while keeping an eye on the river until their turn comes up again. This way everyone gets a chance to cast and work the best water.

I thought about the rotation as I waded through the wobbly rocks, steadying every step with my wading staff, cautiously stopping often and feeling my way around the low, wiry brushes that grew along the margin of the river. Now and then I glanced up at my companion, whose casting continued, immaculate, as it was before. He was well ahead of me now. My D-Loop was too soft and too cautious in normal flows, more so with the strong winds and spatters of rain. I worked out a fair length of the line, made a few casts at a comfortable distance, and began to fish in earnest. But I had forgotten the tough little bushes and smacked my D-Loop right into them. I tugged at the little bush this way and that, but in vain. I had to pick my way back through the slick boulders to free the fly. Then I turned toward the river once again to see how my companion was faring.

"Did you see that fish?" he shouted.

"No, I replied, making another cautious step with my staff. "No, I didn't."

I was surprised by what had happened next. In my home waters in Wisconsin it would be very unusual for one angler to draw another angler's attention to a spot where a fish had shown. Most of the steelhead fishermen I have seen followed the TIMS rule. ("**This is My Spot**, and I can stay here until Hell freezes over.") I have also seen them trading off access among themselves, thereby excluding any intruders.

But not this time. The angler pointed with his rod tip. "Over there," he said. "It came up a few yards upstream, maybe 20 feet out. Looked like a good one."

He was very slightly downstream of the spot he had pointed out, but to him the rotation was in force--it was now my turn to fish through the same water, with the added benefit of knowing where a salmon might be lying. In this instance I could see a rounded hump of fast water near a large boulder, creating a seam of slower water, a pocket several feet long.

Knowing a salmon's position helps, but there are no guarantees in salmon fishing. I swung the big fly through the slot with a strong swimming motion, not a dead drift. On the fifth cast I felt a slow, solid pull--nothing spectacular, but a salmon was hooked up. The big rod bent and throbbed its full length. She rolled to the surface, and I could see she was a bright fish, a few days in the river at most. She did not want to leave that pocket. She stayed within 20 feet of the big boulder field, slugging it out with violent head-shakes. My companion waded out of the river, giving me plenty of room.

"Cold water," he said. "They don't run as far when it's cold."

I knew I would have trouble with the big Spey rod and the slippery boulders. But an angler with 28 years' experience would surely know how to a tail a salmon.

"Would you mind tailing this fish for me? I asked. "I'm not very secure on my feet, and I don't want to beat her up beaching her on these rocks."

He agreed with a nod, propped his rod against a bush, and walked back a bit downstream of the pocket, well downstream of me.

"You'll want to stay back a bit more," I said, grateful for the help. "This is 14-foot rod, and I don't have much experience with it."

The salmon continued to pull, but I had a lot of pressure on. After a few more minutes the salmon rolled again and turned inshore toward the boulders. "I think we can take her now," I said, trying to keep my voice firm and confident.

He moved into deeper water, about knee deep, waited for me to steer the salmon to him, chose his moment, and bent to tail her. He was a tall man with large hands. His left hand closed around the wrist of her tail. In another second his right hand found the pectoral fins, slid under them, and lifted the salmon to the surface--perfect, a textbook performance.

But this salmon did not respond the way the textbook said. She burst from his grasp, the fly came out, she thrashed at the surface for a long moment and was gone.

"Gosh, I'm really sorry," said my companion. "She was bigger than I thought, a very, very nice fish, 15 pounds for sure."

For me a dream of many years had been fulfilled in spectacular fashion, but now I had to respond quickly to reassure him. "In Florida, when the guide touches the leader, that's a caught fish," I said. "I believe the same is true here. And I must say, I'm very grateful to you. You could have cast to that fish yourself, or simply waited until I had fished through, then come in behind me for another try."

I continued hastily to make the point. "This is the first bright Atlantic salmon I have ever caught. It was a gift, and I want to give you a gift in return, something I hope you will use and enjoy."

He started to protest, but I told him that I had co-authored a book on fly-fishing for a tarpon with my guide, Capt. Rob Fordyce, and I would like to send him a copy.

He brightened, nodded, and told me that his grandson was working in Florida and just starting to fish in salt water. He said he would really appreciate such a gift. He wrote out his home address on his business card. I placed his card in my fly box. We shook hands. Then he said he and his wife were expected back at the lodge for lunch. He picked up his rod and started back upstream to the gravel slope, climbed it easily, and disappeared.

The rotation meant a good deal to me now, more than just another stuffy tradition. Then, as I turned away, I saw a heavy splash out in the main current. I noted its position carefully. Then I saw my companion of the past hour drive out onto the bridge. I shouted and waved, but he continued on.

I was wet from a few falls, but I decided I would wade out once again and try to put a fly over the swirl I had seen. But soon the wind began to cut through my wet clothing until I finally gave it up and climbed the gravel slope to my car. The river had risen a few more inches since I first walked down that hill, but I knew where at least one salmon could be found.

Seated inside, with the car heater's fan roaring and rain spattering on the windshield, I thought again about the Rotation, how civil and fair-minded it was, and how I would not have had such a vivid memory to cherish, were it not for this part of the great tradition that is salmon fishing.

Pilgrimage To The Campbell*

In July 1981, I was invited to present a paper at a professional society meeting in Victoria, B.C. My wife and I took advantage of the opportunity and arrived in Victoria a few days early, rented a car, and drove up the coast to Campbell River.

Although I had never visited Vancouver Island before, I had a good idea of what to expect, having read and re-read Roderick Haig-Brown's books about fishing in British Columbia since I was in high school. I knew the "before and after" history of the Campbell River, the names of the famous pools, the big fish that shouldered their way up the river in the fall.

The night clerk at our motel was also a salmon guide, so we made arrangements to go salmon fishing the next morning. I had never mooched for salmon before, but we had a good morning and came back with two nice spring salmon off the Copper Bluffs.

That afternoon, while my wife made arrangements to smoke one of the salmon and have the other fixed for supper, I drove up along the Campbell, stopping briefly to pay my respects at Haig-Brown's home, sad that he had died before I could meet him.

Parking at the trail down the slope to the fly-fishing area, I walked down through the verdant foliage to the Island Pool. I knew there were no fish in the river in mid-July, but I wanted to walk the stream and get the feel of the country. I quickly discovered that what Haig-Brown had written about the slippery rocks was true--one splash of water on the gray-green stones and I fell with a clatter.

I walked downstream about 200 yards, stopping often to watch the water, trying to imagine it in the winter rains, trying to see it as Haig-Brown had. Then I returned to the car, drove back to town, and had a fine dinner of poached salmon with Hollandaise sauce. I felt good about my visit to the river, but I also felt a sense of loss. I had wanted to see that man whose words moved as easily as the river currents.

Later, in the conference center at the University of Victoria, I found myself sitting beneath Haig-Brown's portrait, and while I tried to pay attention to the scholarly papers, I kept thinking about the river. And when the opportunity came to suggest the site for the next conference, I spoke up to suggest that it be held again at Victoria. The proposal passed unanimously and I set my plans in motion for 1984.

One part of my many preparations for the 1984 trip was to write to Erick Carlisle, who in turn referred me to Bob Houton at the fisheries office in Nanaimo. From his staff I learned that one of Haig-Brown's last efforts for conservation on Vancouver Island was to urge the transfer of Tsitika River summer-run steelhead to the Campbell, to protect the strain from logging.

There was at least some hope that these fish would return to the Campbell in 1984. That locked my hopes in place.

On our return to Campbell River in July 1984, we came in our camper and brought our children. As I had done in 1981, we went fishing for salmon in Discovery Passage in the early morning, and though our guide had some motor trouble which cost us an hour of fishing time, we took two bright cohos, and my son felt the power of a nice spring salmon before the hook pulled out near the boat.

After cleaning the morning's salmon, I drove back to the Campbell River, walking down to the river on the same trail to the Island Pool. This time, however, I had a fly rod with me, as well as a wading staff and Dan Bailey's stream cleats--one loss of dignity in 1981 was enough!

The water was low and clear, but I was encouraged by the fact that there were three serious-looking fly fishermen in the upper pool. I waded into the riffle above the lower pool, slipping and sliding into a stable position.

In the best spirit of the occasion, I should have tied on the Silver Brown, but perhaps I will be forgiven for having put up a Green Butt Skunk instead. I had a strange feeling of expectancy, and I remembered from reading A.H.E. Woods *Greased Line Fishing* about casting across the streamy water just below the riffle.

On the first cast, I could see the fly's white wing as it drifted in a slow arc, and suddenly I could also see a gray shape swinging behind it, moving faster. There was a big splash and a tub-sized boil behind the fly, but I felt nothing and didn't strike.

A steelhead! Missed the fly! And I felt a great emptiness at the thought that such a fish, which seemed almost pre-ordained to be there would have missed it. I peered forlornly at the empty water.

It seemed too much to hope that such a fish would come again, but I stayed in the same spot and tried to make the same cast. I couldn't see the fish's lie, couldn't guess where she might have been holding. But I thought if I could make the same cast enough times, she might come again.

So I changed nothing and began to cast across, mending the line once to get the same slow arc, swimming the fly a few inches below the surface. Three casts, four, five-nothing. Then, on the sixth cast, I saw the gray shape again in the green water, just behind the fly, moving a little faster, and I dropped the rod tip to the slow drift.

Again a great splash and boil. The rod yanked down, and the Hardy reel sang that special note, rising to a high whine as the steelhead raced down the river, jumping clear twice.

I was already talking frantically to myself: "Don't fall now! Follow her! Don't try to pressure her yet!" Staff in hand, I began to stumble down the river, hoping that the fish would not reach the tailout and go over.

As I picked my way along, eyes on the bottom, I felt the pressure ease off, and the reel stopped shrieking. I raised the rod prayerfully and began to reel. The backing came in easily, and I felt that awful emptiness again as yard after yard came back on the reel.

Then the steelhead jumped, full out and only 30 feet away. She had come back against the current almost up to the riffle again! Then she shot across the current to the far bank and slugged deep as I caught up to her.

Events of the next several minutes are somewhat muddled now, but I managed to work the steelhead to a gravel shoal, and after a near miss, grasped the wrist of her tail and slid her ashore, the bedraggled Skunk right in the corner of her jaw. Easily 13 lbs., she was bright and unmarked her full length.

Maybe I shouldn't tell you this, but I cried as I freed the hook, took a shaky photograph (the fish wouldn't fit in the viewfinder), and held the great steelhead in the current, moving her back and forth, fearing she would die, hoping she would again feel strong in my hands.

We stayed there in the river together for several minutes as she regained her strength. I could see the wrinkle in her dorsal and the little scar that marked a clipped adipose fin. A hatchery fish, to be sure, but if ever a fish were a tribute to a man's life, this Tsitika River summer steelhead was. Her strain would continue, thanks to Haig-Brown's vision and his ability to inspire a love of rivers in all who would read or listen.

I felt her beginning to pull away, held her little longer, and gave her back to the Campbell.

Study To Be Quiet:
The Heritage of Fly Fishing in the 21st Century

(First given as a speech at the Classic Anglers of Wisconsin Awards Banquet February, 2003.)

Let me first express my thanks for the privilege of speaking here tonight. I've given presentations on fly fishing before, but this is the first time I've had the chance to reflect on the sport of fly fishing as it is today, to acknowledge its historical roots, and to speculate on where it might be going in the

21st century. I'll begin near the beginning of modern fly fishing, in the south of England. Winchester Cathedral stands near the two most famous chalk streams in the world–the River Test and the River Itchen. To me the cathedral's most memorable feature is a stained glass window dedicated to Izaak Walton. It depicts him on the bank of the River Itchen. But he is not fishing or tying on a fly. Instead, he is sitting with his back against a tree, reading a book. Beneath this image are the words "Study To Be Quiet"- a quotation from the *New Testament*, which Walton ends his classic work, *The Compleat Angler*. *The Compleat Angler* and *Dame Juliana Berners'* earlier *Treatyse* begin what we now call the Pastoral Tradition in fishing. Walton frequently remarks on aspects of the English countryside as part of the fishing day--good food and drink, an innocent milkmaid's song, the calls of birds, etc. He describes the very landscape that is depicted in the stained glass window:

Look! Under that broad beech tree I sat down when I as last this way a-fishing. And the birds in the adjoining grove seemed to have a friendly connection with an echo, whose dead voice seemed to live in a hollow tree, near the brow of that primrose hill. There I sat viewing the silver streams glide silently towards their center, the tempestuous sea: yet sometimes opposed by rugged roots and pebble stones, which broke their waves and turned them into foam. And sometimes I beguiled time by viewing the harmless lambs; some leaping securely in the cool shade, whilst others sported themselves in the cheerful sun; and saw others craving comfort from the swollen udders of their bleating dams. As thus I thus sat, these and other sights so full possessed my soul with content, that I thought, as the poet hath happily expressed it, I was for that time lifted above the earth. And possess'd joys not promised in my birth.

The generations of English and American writers that follow Walton sustain and develop the theme of angling as "the contemplative person's recreation." But now, as we face the uncertainties of a new century, we can ask, " What place does Walton's pastoral theme of contemplation and reflection have in our fishing today? Does "Study To Be Quiet" hold any meaning for us? Or is all of this now simply a quaint, half-forgotten part of our history?" At first blush, it seems that we may indeed have forgotten much of our angling heritage. As fishing has become more popular, more accessible, more inclusive, it has also become more competitive. Notice how like each other stock car racing and big-time bass fishing have become. Competitive angling now has a pantheon of heroes who have won millions of dollars in tournaments, whose hats, jackets, and boats proclaim their commercial endorsements.

Yet, for all this attention, they seem quite unable to say anything more insightful than, "Might purty fish!" when yet another bass is boated. Contemplation and insight don't seem to be encouraged very much by metal-flake bass boats, fish locators, autographed lures, and big prize money. There may be some truth in Ted Williams' remark, "I object to fishing tournaments less for what they do to fish than what they do to fishermen."

The pastoral tradition seems also to recede as fishing becomes more and more technical. True, we don't have to spend hundreds of dollars for the latest fish-finding electronics, and a new fly rod is a lot cheaper than, say a new outboard motor. But, to judge from our magazine articles and the advertising that supports them, we have developed an insatiable appetite for the latest gadgets and technical innovations.

Flies used to bear romantic names as part of the pastoral tradition, such as *Pale Morning Dun, Silver Doctor, Queen of the Waters* or *Iron Blue Dun*. Flies were also named for famous people and places in angling, such as the *Lady Beaverkill*, the *Henryville Caddis*, the *Seth Green, Wickham's Fancy*, and the *Royal Wulff*. There is a curious pleasure simply in reciting such wonderful names, and they used to number in the hundreds as part of the lore of fly fishing.

Nowadays, quasi-scientific names predominate--the romantic *Pale Morning Dun* becomes *PMD Emerger*, the Speckled-Wing Dun is now the *Callibaetis*, the *Blue-Winged Oliver* is now the *BWO Cripple*, or to be more scientific and politically correct, the *Baetis Challenged*. (I'm not kidding, check the Cabela's catalogue!) Or what about "*Flav*" a cute nickname for *Emphemerella flavilinea*, once known as the Blue Quill?

There are other, even less attractive names that straight from zap-'em video games, such as *Purple Egg-Sucking Electric Leech*, or *Black Rubber-Legged Conehead Crystal Bugger*. (I wouldn't want to meet one of those on a rainy night!) Or consider the foam plastic "fly," the *Chernobyl Ant*, evoking a radioactive mutant deformity from a nuclear disaster.

We also want faster and more painless ways of learning the essential skills of fly fishing. Long ago, a father or an uncle might have taught us to cast, or perhaps we learned from a book. It was slow and often discouraging. But mastering it distinguished us from other anglers--an exclusive mystique surrounded us. Now we can choose among a variety of casting videos by Federation-certified instructors, or we can pay a few hundred dollars to attend a weekend fly-fishing school. If we're lucky, and we all are here in Wisconsin, a nearby fly shop will offer casting lessons. It's all so easy now– or so it seems.

In the virtual reality of video we can peer over the shoulders of expert fly-tiers as they demonstrate their skills, rather than learning slowly and often painfully from other anglers or a tattered *Herter's* manual. Instead of exploring new water on our own, with much trial and error, we can buy stream-specific guidebooks and hatch charts. But I wonder if the videos, the weekend fishing schools, the hatch charts and the guidebooks do much to develop our capacity for observation and reflection--to learn the songs of birds along with the double haul or the puddle cast, to learn to love home waters as much as the fabulous destinations half a world away.

Will the pastoral tradition in fly fishing survive hatch charts, or genetically engineered hackles, and higher-modulus rod blanks? Or is the fly-fishing contest in ESPN's Great Outdoor Games a better indicator of what is to come? Will fly fishing become just another spectator sport, with a yearly "Flymaster Classic"?

I had occasion to think about all this a few years ago. In a landscape very like Walton's English countryside, on one of our spring creeks, I saw a trout rise near an undercut bank. As I made ready to cast, a blackbird with bright red epaulets flew low over the pool and spooked the fish out of the open water and back under the bank. It was a nice one, and there were some blue-winged olives--Sorry, I mean some *Baetis*--coming off, so I decided to sit there and wait to see if it would resume feeding.

To pass the time, I took inventory of my gear. I had on a pair of synthetic leather wading boots, Gore-Tex waders, a recycled fiber vest, Supplex shirt, and DEET bug repellent. I had a 2 ½-ounce third-generation graphite fly rod, PVC plastic-coated line, copolymer leader tippet, and a parachute dry fly tied of Micro Fibbetts, genetically engineered hackle, synthetic fiber dubbing, and polypropylene yarn wing post, tied on a chemically sharpened hook. Almost everything in my outfit was made of unpronounceable artificial molecules whose half-life is probably much longer than mine.

Sitting there among the nodding violets, I recalled a long-ago day on another stream, full of tradition, where I was determined to use traditional tackle--bamboo rod, silk line, gut leader, etc. But my traditional silk fly line sank at just the wrong moment, despite enough Mucilin on it to float a grindstone. My carefully soaked 4X gut leader tippet broke at random, and the bottle containing my traditional paraffin and gasoline fly flotant leaked, leaving an evil-smelling stain on my poplin fishing vest, right next to the 6-12 bug dope stain.

The 14-inch brown trout I caught that day now seems almost a miracle. But my tackle would have met a high technical standard in the 1950s.

Meanwhile, the trout I was waiting for had resumed feeding. My plastic-coated four-weight fly line cast easily and floated high, and my copolymer tippet and chemically sharpened hook held fast when the fish jumped and ran into the undercut. As I released the trout near its hole under the bank, itself the product of many hours of hard volunteer work, I realized that my modern equipment had helped me to catch a trout I probably could not have caught 50 years ago. Indeed, the trout itself would probably not have been there, since the landowner's cows were accustomed to watering nearby and had broken down the already heavily eroded stream banks. Now the erosion is gone, the banks are protected with sturdy fences, and the stream runs clear and cold.

Can the pastoral tradition survive our fascination with the modern trappings of high-tech graphite rods, AST-coated fly lines, fluorocarbon leaders, and the infinite complexities of modern fly tying? I think it can, because, though hushed to a murmur, it is still with us, most clearly in the stories we tell. Most of the anglers I know enjoy telling their own stories and reading or listening to the stories of others, and in the telling, recasting their tales in what Flip Pallot has called "the alchemy of recollection," wherein the base metal of raw experience is transformed into golden memories.

Such is the nature of human experience, that our capacity to recollect events is defined and framed by our common fly fishing heritage. All of us feel part of that heritage, that we have embarked upon a special journey, something quite different from other forms of fishing--more a way of life than a sport. And I think our awareness of the pastoral tradition is revealed most clearly in our own alchemy of recollection.

My recent efforts to tell the stories of adventures in tarpon fishing are noted by my readers more often than the technical material, often beginning with "You know that part where you lost your entire leader because your nail knot slipped? Well, the same thing happened to me one time. . ." and he's off retelling his own story, with dramatic gestures and sound effects. This story-telling is at the heart of angling, even though it is often hidden beneath the how-to/where-to stuff.

Angling books of the past speak often and at great length about preparing lines, lures, scents and attractants, etc. Walton explains how to tie an artificial fly, how to bait a hook with a big lobworm or a cased caddis larva, how to keep live baits fresh and wholesome, how to make and dye a twisted horsehair line. Though nowhere near his friend Charles Cotton's skill at fly fishing, he describes twelve fly patterns and a dubious technique for a drag-free float--walking the bank at the same speed as the current.

It's obvious Walton wasn't much of a fly fisherman. Truth to tell, he writes with more authority about using live mayflies and fuzzy caterpillars as bait. But he accords a special stature to fly fishing:

O sir, doubt not that angling is an art. Is it not an art to deceive a trout with an artificial fly? A trout! that is more sharp-sighted than any hawk you have named, and more watchful and timorous than your high-mettled merlin is bold; and yet I doubt not to catch a brace or two tomorrow for a friend's breakfast; doubt not therefore, sir, but that angling is an art, and an art worth your learning. The question is rather, whether you be capable of learning it? For angling is somewhat like poetry, men are to be born so: I mean, with inclinations to it, though both may be heightened by discourse and practice; but he that hopes to be a good angler, must not only bring an inquiring, searching, observing wit, but he must bring a large measure of hope and patience, and a love and propensity to the art itself; but having once got and practiced it, then doubt not but angling will prove to be so pleasant, that it will prove to be like virtue, a reward to itself.

Walton's contemporaries often made their own rods, lines, and flies, and he takes obvious delight in the intricacies of baits and tackle. Modern fly fishers don't have to build their rods or tie their own flies, but many do, and their delight in being part of the tradition of craftsmanship is at least as great as his. There is rapidly growing enthusiasm for building rods of traditional split bamboo. Fly-tiers of my acquaintance tie hundreds of flies, most of which will never see action. Nevertheless, they take great pleasure in collecting materials, learning new techniques, and thumbing through pattern books. It's a wonder they can find any time to go fishing. Furled leaders are back in vogue after 200 years, and steelhead anglers have rediscovered the pleasures of casting long two-handed Spey rods.

The pastoral tradition may be obscured by the popularity of how-to books and videos, but it has had vigorous expression by modern American writers such as Ted Leeson, Russell Chatham, Seth Norman, John Cole, Steve Raymond, Tom McGuane, and, of course, Norman Maclean-not to mention the landmark film he inspired. And there is Flip Pallot's *Walker's Cay Chronicles* on ESPN, a bright spot in an often tedious array of televised fishing shows.

As I look ahead to the 21st century, to the ever increasing human population, continuing threats to our watersheds, and the rapid privatization of streams and lakes, I am aware of the dangers we face, but I am convinced that, to survive as a sport, we must give more attention to the thoughtful aspects of fly fishing that nurture our souls, and breathe new life into our traditions for the next generation. I don't know exactly how to do this, but I'm sure that stories are part of it.

At the same time--and this is the hard part--we cannot forget or paper over the fact that, no matter how much it might be refined, no matter how frequently we invoke the catch and release ethic, fishing is a blood sport. Most of the people in this room began our angling careers by catching a fish that we kept and ate. Many of us were attracted to fly fishing not only because it was effective--often more effective than any other method.

Fascinating as the art of fly fishing is, with all its wonderful tools and the graceful flow of the cast, it is still a way to catch fish, sometimes to eat. There is something--something stronger than mere sentiment--that connects us to the animals we hunt or fish for. Casual hikers and weekend boaters do not know this deep attachment, but hunters and fishermen do, and it is the basis for their willingness to contribute money and countless hours of effort to protect them and their habitat. To deny this is not only to overlook a fundamental dimension of human nature; it opens the way to those who argue that catch and release fishing is merely another way of tormenting other creatures to gratify ourselves, like cock-fighting or bull-baiting. And I fear their ranks are increasing faster than ours. We, who are already committed to fly fishing as a sport and as a way of life, have an opportunity here, at Fly Fish Wisconsin and in our local fly-fishing clubs, to acquaint others with that we have known, to tell our stories even as we help them learn the skills of fly fishing- - our angling heritage, to know those sublime moments in fly fishing--to learn that there is much more to fishing than fish. Who knows, if we refocus our attention on the most gratifying aspects of fly fishing, we might encounter an angler sitting near a good pool reading a book. If you do, take another look, it could be me, Studying To Be Quiet. But also keep in mind that in his famous window Walton is depicted not only with a book in hand, but with his rod and his empty creel at the ready, waiting for a rise. In closing, I'd like to leave you with a favorite Walton quote that seems appropriate to this occasion, betraying a sentiment less than saintly but for that all the more genuine. At least I think there's a lot of truth in it:

These, my honest scholar, are some observations told to you as they now come suddenly into my memory, of which you may make some use; but for the practical part, it is this that makes an angler; it is diligence, and observation, and practice, and an ambition to be the best in the art, that must do it. I will tell you, scholar, I once heard one say, *"I envy not him that eats better meat than I do, nor him that is richer, or that wears better clothes than I do; I envy nobody but him, and him only, that catches more fish than I do." And such a man is like to prove an angler; and this noble emulation I wish to you and all young anglers.*

*Pilgrimage to the Campbell

Reprinted from August-September, 1987, *Salmon Trout Steelheader* magazine,
Frank Amato Publications.